The DEVON ORCHARDS Book

HALSGROVE

CPRE Devon
Campaign to Protect Rural England

First published in Great Britain in 2018

Copyright © Michael Gee

All rights reserved. No part of this publication may be reproduced, stored in a retrieval system, or transmitted in any form or by any means without the prior permission of the copyright holder.

British Library Cataloguing-in-Publication Data
A CIP record for this title is available from the British Library

ISBN 978 0 85704 310 8

HALSGROVE
Halsgrove House,
Ryelands Business Park,
Bagley Road, Wellington, TA21 9PZ
Tel: 01823 653777   Fax: 01823 216796
email: sales@halsgrove.com

Part of the Halsgrove group of companies
Information on all Halsgrove titles is available at: www.halsgrove.com

Printed and bound by Parksons Graphics, India

Contents

Foreword 5
Acknowledgements 7

1 Introduction 9
2 Against the Odds 13
3 Exotic Origins..19
4 Medieval Decision-Making 25
5 Moving into the Modern Era 33
6 Devon Orchards and the Cider Explosion 43
7 Cider Country 53
8 Seeds of Decline 61
9 Near Disappearance..69
10 Devon's Orchard Heritage 83
11 Revival and the Future..101
12 The Future 131

Appendix 1 140
Appendix 2 141
References 143

Autumn at Poltimore Orchard, Farway, near Colyton. (Tim Potter)

Foreword

As Chairman of the Devon branch of CPRE (The Campaign to Protect Rural England), I'm delighted that we have sponsored the production of this new book by Michael Gee on the traditional orchards of Devon, and the old varieties of apples which were once widely grown here.

Michael's meticulous research to record the county's fruit-growing history is a wonderful example of what we strive to do at CPRE Devon – preserve our rural way of life, and all that is precious about our county and our countryside, for future generations to benefit from.

CPRE Devon campaigns for well-planned development to enable the people of Devon to live and work, to develop new businesses, and to continue to contribute to the nation's economy, but without having to sacrifice all of the more traditional aspects of our way of life.

Ancient knowledge and traditions can so easily be lost if not committed to paper. The painstaking work of enthusiasts like Michael Gee preserve it for future generations. This book demonstrates how the knowledge of our forebears, far from being forgotten, can be used to inspire and benefit new enterprises in our region, whilst simultaneously reviving the cultivation and use of our traditional apple varieties.

Recent years have seen a renaissance in micro brewing and artisanal cider making as people seek an alternative to the bland, mass-produced drinks commonly available in our supermarkets, and many of our pubs. We hope that readers of this book will be inspired to spread the word about Devon's very special part in the history of British orchards.

Rebecca Bartleet, CPRE Devon

Acknowledgements

After writing a short book on mazzards around the Millennium a number of people asked me why I had not tackled the bigger subject of Devon's orchards. After a decade of mulling over the idea I decided that a short book of case studies might be revealing. I started talking to people about the idea, talked to my publisher and was eventually approached by CPRE. It has taken quite a time, and the book that has emerged is rather different from the one I started.

Over the course of a number of years I have talked to many scores of people. I cannot think of a case of difficulty or unpleasantness, even when I've called at an orchard unexpectedly. When I've arrived I've often been asked to jump in a Land Rover and been taken to it. I don't think this is me, I think it must be something to do with Devonians and particularly those who are associated with orchards or research.

I cannot name scores of people here, even if at my age I could recall them all. I should just like to acknowledge and embrace everybody in my thanks.

The committees and members of Orchards Live, Orchards Link and the Tamar & Tavy Apple Group were all supportive. Long Ashton must have been a special place; the former staff could not have been more helpful.

Fruit growers, cider makers and other users were patient and helpful in answering all my questions, often when there was work to be done.

Information held at the museums or heritage centres at Braunton, Colyton, Devon Rural Archive, Kingsbridge, Sidmouth and Whimple, as well as that held by National Trust and Devon Wildlife Trust, was made readily available; thanks so much.

Staff and helpers at SW Heritage Trust (Barnstaple and Exeter), Devon and Exeter Institution and Devon Garden History Society made visits to their libraries a pleasure.

Thanks to the photographers who helped – I had expected to be overwhelmed but wasn't.

Other authors and researchers were generous with their time and assistance. And if you don't fit into any of the above categories (and I can think if some who don't), it doesn't mean you're overlooked.

A grant from the Steel Charitable Trust to Dartington North Devon Trust to assist the Orchards Live photography archive had a most helpful spin-off. The support of CPRE is very thankfully acknowledged; otherwise there might have been a very meagre book or none at all. I am most grateful to both.

Michael Gee
Landkey, July 2018

Fruitful standard orchard at harvest time, Efford, Shute (near Crediton).

Ch 1
Introduction

'The orchard walls are high and hard to climb'
(William Shakespeare, Romeo and Juliet)

'A facetious stranger observed that "if it were only for its cream and butter, Devonshire might be termed an earthly paradise"; we should add that its fruits equally entitle it to so proud a name' (Rachel Evans, 1846)

Orchards became important to me in childhood when my father broke down the wall that separated our family garden from an abandoned neighbouring one; we clambered through the hole and entered our new orchard. It was part of a large Victorian garden that had become available after subdivision, – a few very old trees provided a secret world for tree climbing, camping, bonfires and picking 'Beauty of Bath' apples in the holidays.

It was a long time later that I moved to Devon, (in 1987), and soon found myself inaugurating a Save our Orchards Campaign in North Devon which evolved into Orchards Live. I thank Common Ground for the inspiration.

I found that Rachel Evans's image of a county of orchards and fruit complementing the cows and cream was not matched by reality. Only a relatively lucky few Devonians eat fruit grown in the county or drink cider and juice from a local orchard, and who could name a Devon variety or locate their nearest orchard? So there's a disconnection and a paradox; there was support and enthusiasm for the Campaign based on very limited knowledge.

Devon has lost out to other counties in terms of cider making and orchards. In recent years this situation has been changing. The decline in orchards appears to have 'bottomed out'. There are some large modern orchards and new cider makers. There has been a growing awareness of the importance of orchards, with many individuals and some communities restoring them or planting new ones, sometimes with public help. Nurserymen are able to supply varieties of Devon fruit which had almost disappeared. 'Provenance' and 'craft' have become important in the sale of food and drink, and are encouraging local initiatives. This story of Devon orchards' origins, rise, fall and recent revival is interesting and needs telling.

Batson Valley, near Salcombe. (Kingsbridge Cookworthy Museum)

Blossom at Berry Pomeroy. (Peter Rodd)

The literature on Devon's orchards is thin. There are books on different fruit varieties, dealing with origin, cultivation and use. There are technical books on orchard management. The county and its cider makers have stimulated some poetic literature. There are all sorts of materials on the web. But books on Devon's orchards in the round, dealing with their history, wildlife, landscape significance, place in the local community, uses, and contribution to the local economy in the widest sense, don't exist. It was only in the 1990s that the Campaign started opening people's eyes to the many different ways in which orchards are, or should be, important to us all. Two or three decades isn't very long for a literature to develop.

We need to start with a definition, but advance with care. On so many occasions I have been asked whether a person's small collection of trees qualifies as an orchard, and I don't like to disappoint. Orchards are organised collections of free-standing cultivated fruit trees. I don't think their areal size matters, but in terms of numbers it is likely to be more than two or three to be described as a collection. In Devon

INTRODUCTION

The Word 'Orchard'

The word orchard is defined as 'a piece of enclosed land planted with fruit trees' or just as 'an area devoted to the cultivation of fruit trees'. Some definitions add nuts to fruit, others exclude citrus fruits (which are grown in groves). There is agreement that orchards have planted trees (not bushes); how many trees is an open debate.

But the word has not always been used so precisely. It is probably derived from the Old English and/or Latin words for plant and yard: wort/hortus and geard. The word orcead might have been moving to the modern meaning at the end of the Saxon period. So possibly at the time of the origins of the English language there were no orchards as we know them today. Fruit trees were not planted to grow by themselves but were part of plant yards, or what we might also call gardens.

Expressions like 'apple gardens' were still in common usage in the early modern period. North Devon's mazzards are grown in gardens, grounds and closes, not orchards. In Landkey I was corrected for saying 'mazzard orchard'; 'It's a garden' I was told. There is a welcoming arch to the mazzard trees on Landkey's Millennium Green; 'Mazzard Orchard' it says: modern times!

It will be argued that only over course of time were fruit trees grown by themselves, and an old word acquired a new meaning.

about 99% of the fruits are varieties of apple, with pears, plums and cherries accounting for nearly all the rest. I say organised and free-standing because the trees need to have been planted in a certain way – seedlings on an old railway embankment, 'ballerina' trees in pots or a hedge of espaliered trees may be fascinating, but aren't orchards.

I used the adjective 'cultivated' because a collection of wild trees isn't an orchard. By cultivation I mean most orchards contain fruits of known varieties grafted or budded onto rootstocks to determine size and form, supplied by a nurseryman. They are very different from, say, ancient woodland.

Using this definition there are over 2000 orchards in Devon, with perhaps 35,000 in England as a whole. Their products of food and drink provide livelihoods for hundreds and pleasure for hundreds of thousands. Blossom in spring and fruit-bearing boughs in autumn provide visual delight; many are invaluable playgrounds. Clumps of orchard trees in unlikely places, particularly nestling amongst farm buildings or on village edges can be an important asset in the appearance of the landscape. The wildlife value of old orchards is now recognised, and if the Devonshire orchard management regime is not always entirely rigorous, so much the better.

An underlying theme in the book is the challenge of growing fruit. Devon is on the margin. Thus success is particularly satisfying, and this satisfaction needs to be shared. Devon's orchards need to be better understood and appreciated, and this will give them a better place in the future.

Luscombe drinks promote an attractive orchard image.
(P. Rodd)

11

Orchard planted by Chris Niesigh in sheltered steep-sided valley, Combe Martin.

Ch 2
Against the Odds

The title of this chapter might surprise. While in British terms Devon might be considered a favoured county for agriculture and horticulture, only in limited areas is it suitable for fruit growing that can compete with other parts of the country or parts of the world. A study of orchard fruit growing world-wide puts UK's main fruit, apples, around fortieth place. For apples China, USA, Turkey, Poland, India and Italy head the list. For other orchard fruits (pears, plums, cherries) the UK comes even lower down. In Europe Austria, Belgium, France, Germany, Hungary, Spain, Switzerland and Ukraine, as well as already-mentioned Italy, all produce greater quantities of fruit than the UK. Within the UK the main areas for fruit production are Kent, Worcestershire and Herefordshire. Others are more significant than Devon which is relatively a modest producer.

Why should this be? Writing in Devon, Ben Pike says 'There is such a thing as a perfect site for growing fruit trees. It would be a south-facing spot sheltered from strong winds and away from frost pockets. The soil would be fertile, well-drained loam with a pH of around 6.5. Although such sites are to be found, it is unlikely that you will live in such a place' (Pike). To which might be added, 'particularly in Devon'. I remember visiting a well-known orchard owner and drinks maker who boasted smugly that an orchard expert had once told him that there were few ideal spots for orchard growing in the South West and that he had one of them; it wasn't in Devon.

So how does Devon match up to Ben Pike's requirements? Very few farmers anywhere have perfect conditions for doing what they do, but they make the best of prevailing conditions. We need to say a few words about

The orchard planted by Chris Niesigh in Combe Martin.

geology, topography, soils and climate plus other considerations that might make an area successful for fruit growing. And we shouldn't expect the whole of Devon to meet the requirements: even when orchard acreage was at its greatest there were just 15,610 ha (38,592 acres) in the county, representing about 2.55% of the total land area.

Geology

Geologically, Devon is mostly made up of rocks of Devonian and Carboniferous age (395-280 million years old). The Devonian age left rocks mainly formed in desert conditions (Old Red Sandstone), while the Carboniferous age is characterised by marine deposition (shales and sandstones of the Culm Measures). Around 290 million years ago there were volcanic intrusions and metamorphism. In the east of the county are also found younger (280-230 million years ago) Permian rocks (New Red Sandstone). Subsequently sea cover left deposits which have been removed by erosion except for tiny fragments of Jurassic and Cretaceous deposition in the extreme south-east. Generally speaking this is the surface geology we have today. There are significant clay deposits from the Tertiary era. Climate changes in the last two million years (the Quaternary era), including severe cold, have led to modifications of slopes and alterations to the coast as sea level has changed.

Topography

Challenged to describe the relief of Devon in one sentence, one might say that it is an exposed plateau dissected by combes and river valleys which are flooded by the sea in the south. In the north there is a hilly plateau of Devonian bedrocks, about 250m-250m, at its highest on Exmoor. Devon is rich in slopes. North of the line of the old Barnstaple to Dulverton railway there are many over 5 degrees with ridges and hillcrests on a west-east alignment. On the Carboniferous Culm Measures there are fewer slopes over 5 degrees – this is a landscape of an undulating plateau with broader valleys. The centre of the county is dominated by the volcanic intrusion of Dartmoor. Slope alignment to the east is southwest to northeast. South of the moor, with the slates, mudstones and sandstones of the Devonian bedrocks, slopes of 5 degrees or more again follow a broadly west-east alignment, except where dissected by the drainage system's north-south drowned valleys. There are estuaries and rivers, and where these river valleys are flooded there can be navigation a long way inland (Friend).

Fruit can grow on much higher land than is found in Devon. Far more critical than altitude are aspect and exposure. The ideal conditions for fruit are often said to be south-facing gently sloping sites. While the common west-

Ash invasion at Pippacott, Braunton.

east relief meets these needs, fruit also needs shelter from winds, particularly to ensure good pollination, and the pattern of relief does not provide this.

Soils

Orchards can be created on a range of soils. Apples do best on fertile, well-drained loams. Rootstocks have been developed to suit different conditions, but cannot overcome the problems of poorly drained soils, of which there are plenty in Devon. The lack of aeration inhibits root development, so that trees take up less nutrients, affecting tree and crop size; trees can also be less stable and more susceptible to diseases like crown rot.

With a complex underlying geology, as well as variations in climate, altitude, slope aspect and centuries of human modification, Devon has an enormous complexity of soils over small areas, and farmers will tell you how one field is quite different to another. The soils of the two moors are acid, with a lot of peat on Dartmoor. The Culm Measures (across central northern Devon) and the Blackdown Hills have wet, acid soils. Mid and East Devon Devon have

AGAINST THE ODDS

Apple tree resilience, Cockington. (Tim Potter)

establishment in southern combes.

John Bradbeer has looked at the distribution of orchards on the Culm Measures as shown in the mid nineteenth century Tithe Survey, with significantly more on the Culm Measures to the south and west of Barnstaple than on the Devonian rocks of Exmoor and its foothills. Climatic and soil conditions played a part in the distribution of orchards with areas of the Culm Measures with cold soils and high rainfall having fewer orchards than other areas of Culm Measures with better drained soils (Bradbeer).

Wind exposure at Fairlinch, Braunton. (Tim Potter)

slightly acid loams and clays. The soils of the South Hams are slightly acid and free draining.

'Soil providing less than 40cm of unrestricted rooting will stunt tree growth' stressed Ray Williams. There is also the risk that waterlogging will cause tree damage or even death. Where depth is due to compaction cultivation may remedy the situation, but otherwise shallow soils are not for orchards.

The question of drainage is particularly important for apple trees, and there are parts of the county that are unsuitable. The old adage is that trees don't like wet feet, and trees in poorly drained flat fields often struggle. Sometimes trees were planted on artificial ridges or mounds, and adding organic matter can improve poorly drained soils. However, drainage problems rarely restrict orchard

Climate

In world terms, England is marginal when it comes to fruit growing, because of its climate. Orchards need direct summer sun and humidity. Winter chilling is important, as is avoidance of frosts at blossom time. Strong winds at blossoming and harvest are bad news

Devon is wet (most of the county west of the Exe has over 1000mm rainfall per annum), but the important point is the huge rainfall gradient over short distances. The climate is also warm and mild (the maritime influence),

Misty autumn morning, Whimple.

Frosty morning, Whimple.

leading to a long growing season. It is sunshine lack (with reduced fruit sugars) that is more critical than temperature. Winter chill for 'vernalisation' and frost for pest control are some years lacking, but not strong winds. All these characteristics are not necessarily good news for the fruit grower, and explain why growing is 'against the odds'. Thus Devon can be considered more marginal than other parts of England. Its climate suits apples more than plums (lack of sun can reduce crop and humidity increases disease), or pears (lack of sun).

It is the links between topography and climate that are the main determinants of Devon's suitability for orchards. Certain climatic disadvantages can be overcome: careful siting on sunny and well drained slopes, alignment of planting, shelter belts, avoidance of frost pockets are all examples of ways in which orchard friendly micro-climates can be produced.

Climatic changes are forecast, but the impact on Devon's orchards is a matter of speculation. If orchards place in the county's husbandry is marginal, then there will certainly need to be adjustments.

CLIMATE CHANGE

Changes in climate in historical times have affected fruit growing in Devon. For the last few decades there has been global warming largely attributed to greenhouse gases. 'We can now conclude with a high degree of confidence that the world will become hotter, but it will be extreme events – such as heavy rainstorms combined with long periods of drought – that will present the greatest challenges to society' (Webster).

Projected temperature changes for Devon show rises in seasonal mean temperature of over 3 degrees C in the winter and over 2 degrees C in the summer by the 2080s. For Devon's orchards frost-free winters, particularly a succession of them, would be a significant change. Extreme events, particularly storms and periods of very heavy rainfall, are already a feature of Devon's climate, but more of them will be a challenge to fruit growers. Occasional droughts, accentuated by higher summer temperatures and soils, will be another.

> **CANKER**
>
> Canker and scab are the two most serious fruit diseases in Devon. Scab is a fungal infection of apples and pears linked to the wet temperate climate of the county. Cankers in plums and cherries are often described as bacterial rather than fungal in origin.
>
> Apples and pears can be affected when the spores enter cuts, and this is most likely when trees are wet during and after rainfall. Release of spores varies; that in summer affects the fruit, that at leaf fall in the autumn affects the trees. Damage to fruit (through rot) and young trees makes the problem serious.
>
> The problem should not be exaggerated. Many varieties are resistant (though not immune), and many traditional Devon varieties fall into this category. New varieties have been bred to resist the disease. Through careful observation and good orchard practices the problem can be controlled or treated. Those planting new trees should make themselves well aware of the problem.
>
> There is ongoing research into whether climate change will encourage the disease and indeed whether the disease is itself changing and becoming more virulent.

Population and Markets

Any county will only produce as much fruit as it can consume or take to market. So Kent's fruit growing has been attributed to the London market (historically via Gravesend), while Hereford and the West Country turned to cider making because was easier to transport to market (Roach). Trying to establish Devon's population changes from medieval to modern times, with reference to national picture, is not easy. Jonathan Barry goes through the problems and points out that W.G. Hoskins never attempted precise totals. An estimate for 1660 is 227,157 out of England's total of 5.1million (Barry). There was 58% growth by 1805, with Devon's total reaching 358,987. The population of Exeter has been estimated as between 7500 and 8500 in 1520, and by 1660 had reached around 12,000, half as much again (MacCaffrey). There has to be a relationship between population and fruit growing. If the population is low, so would be the amount of fruit growing. Low rural and town populations until Elizabethan times were followed by growth along with growth of domestic and overseas trade, but Devon remained a long way from substantial markets.

Communications

It needs to be emphasised how poor a lot of local communication was until recently: Cecil Torr's delightful *Small Talk at Wreyland* is an account of Devon life a century or so ago, and has vivid accounts of how the packhorse was only replaced by wheeled transport relatively recently. Coastal areas and estuaries of the south favoured orchards because fruit could be shipped out, and cider was taken by boat to London and other parts. But topography and poor communication meant that orchard products would in the main be serving very localised markets until the arrival of the railways.

However, Devon was well placed for Overseas Trade, and we will argue that the county's position in relation to this trade enabled the provision of cider to ships, sailors, traders and colonists which stimulated the planting of orchards on a considerable scale. Much later Whiteways were able to develop a national market from Devon because of railways, showing that entrepreneurial spirit can overcome the marginal disadvantages of geography. The company's advertising put a strong emphasis on the healthiness of a drink made from beautiful fruit from a beautiful county.

So while 'Against the Odds' might be a fair summary of Devon's physical conditions for developing orchards, it has to be admitted that Devonians have over the centuries been ingenious in establishing and maintaining them, and quite a few have triumphed against the odds. But the underlying marginality of Devon's orchards in today's global world has to be recognised.

Ch 3
Exotic Origins

Those who talk about 'native' English woodlands are often surprised to learn that many common trees are recent introductions. So it is with orchards, but more so. When it comes to Devon's orchards the trees that grow in them are not 'native' at all. The four commonest fruits historically are apples, pears, plums and cherries. Apples originated in western China and pears in the same area, while plums are from Eastern Europe and the Caucasus, with cherries coming from Southern Europe. Most apples, pears and plums are introductions in historical times. Mazzards could have been domesticated locally. Only tiny numbers of other fruits are found growing in Devon's orchards. So how and when were they introduced?

Apples

We have to start with the story of the apple, and actually the story of two apples: wild apples and domesticated apples. The Latin name for apple, Malus, is the name of a genus of up to fifty species. From earliest times there has been a wild apple species growing in Britain, Malus sylvestris, known as the crab apple. The important point is that while the tree fruits, and its fruits can be used, they are small and hard, hence the adjective 'crabby'. They have never been domesticated into the larger apples that are found in Devon's orchards. Orchard apples are of another species, Malus pumila.

When the apple on the front cover of Pete Brown's recent book is described as 'our most English fruit' does he mean 'English by adoption'? The genus Malus probably arose in the Tertiary Era in southern China (Juniper). It spread throughout a continuous corridor of temperate forest as far west as Western Europe. But this corridor has since been fragmented, leaving Malus sylvestris widely distributed across Europe and native to these islands, frequenting hedgerows, copses and woodlands and occasionally finding their way into place names, such as the legendary Avalon in Somerset. In prehistoric times crabs were eaten, and probably fermented into cider, but because of their small size, hard texture, bitter taste and seasonality, it is hard to regard them as a significant contributor to Devon's diet. Today they are foraged for use in jellies, and occasionally for wine. Orchards are not planted with Malus sylvestris but the tree may be planted as a pollinator, or used as a rootstock. So we can say that crab apples have little to do with Devon orchards. However this does not mean that there is not a widely held, but fundamentally wrong, myth that there is some sort of continuity from the crab apples probably growing on the Isle of Avalon and the orchards of the West Country today.

The fact is that the domesticated apple we grow in orchards today, Malus pumila, has been introduced from Asia, and the story is a fascinating one and bears repeating.

One of the products of the fragmentation of the Malus population in Tertiary times, referred to above, has been the relict fruit forest of the Tian Shan in China. 'It transpires that only in the great ranges of the Tian Shan of Xinjiang Uygur of western China to Uzbekistan were all the

Opposite: Dog with apples, Orchard Farm, Cheriton Fitzpaine. (Tim Potter)

conditions – geological, meteorological, tectonic, pedological, and ecological, plus very long periods of relatively undisturbed time – consistently present to drive forward the evolution of the large sweet apple of the supermarket shelf from its tiny bird-distributed ancestors' (Juniper). These mountains are the result of the Indian subcontinent's tectonic plate colliding with the mass of Asia, leading to the Himalayas, and the Tian Shan. It is dry, but the surrounding areas are drier, closing it off in almost all directions. Still subject to uplift and geological distortion the area is one of constantly rejuvenated soils. And while glaciations in much of the northern hemisphere had a devastating effect on plant life, 'in eastern Asia, with increasing northern cold, the Tertiary temperate and tender plants were able to retreat south or spread away from locally developing mountain ice packs without serious restriction and to recolonize as conditions improved. Crop plants, or their ancestors, were still present in the Kasakh-Uzbec area, hence the stimulus to domesticate equines there. At the same time, the powerful monsoon influence kept at bay, to an extent, the continentality of climate. Inner and eastern Asia, over many millions of years in the key period for flowering plant evolution, that is, from about 100 million years ago, were able to retain and develop a richness of flora denied to western Europe or North America' (Juniper).

There are many questions about the precursors of Malus pumila in the Tian Shan. Whatever their origins, there are fruit forests of wild populations of Malus pumila whose seed could not easily be spread north, west or south because of hostile arid terrain. But there was a corridor to the west, and Juniper argues that bears, selecting larger fruit, spread their seed through defecation. Bears, horses, camels, dung beetles and finally men have all played their part in this fascinating story. Movements of man, pack horses (a horse's gut might take an apple pip 40 miles) and primitive trade along the Turkic corridor are huge unknowns, but they are all part of the westward movement. We know for sure that there were apples in ancient Mesopotamia, and Malus pumila had reached the Mediterranean by the reign of Ramesses II (1279-1213BC). Thence it reached the classical world, and with the Romans into Britain.

But here another huge question is begged. If the apples advanced westwards over thousands of years exclusively in the form of seedlings, the progeny would have been varied, from the edible to the impossibly astringent. Apples are self-incompatible, and as all who have tried to sow an apple pip know, the high degree of polymorphism means that the resulting tree seldom resembles the parents. So the earliest farmers must have experimented with other forms of propagation. Cuttings and layering seldom work, and the result was grafting – we don't know where or when, but we know that the practice has been around for thousands of years.

And now an aside that is pertinent to Devon. Juniper says that there is little stimulus for the development of grafting as long as there is a rich diversity of fecund seedling growth. 'Every roadside fruit stall in Uzbekistan, Kyrgyzstan, and Kazakhstan displays a cornucopia of apples in season. But enquiries as to the name of the cultivar will be met with confusion and the explanation that any particularly choice apple comes from somewhere up an adjacent valley. Why be concerned with time-wasting

Selecting grafting material at Scion Day, Eggesford.

EXOTIC ORIGINS

propagation when diversity prevails, and when a favoured apple tree dies there are so many to take its place?' (Juniper). Could this argument also apply to Devon with the scattering of discarded pomace, sometimes as pig food? There was more incentive to develop grafting in arid conditions.

The antiquity of grafting often surprises people. So this practice, known to Egyptians, Persians, Greeks, Romans, Celts – when would it have been known in Devon? What is more surprising to me is the way that the practice has featured in illustration, not only in often copied Roman mosaics in Gaul, but in Cirencester where Pomona is shown wielding a pruning knife.

So there can be no doubt that in the villa culture of Roman Britain there would be grafted apple trees of Malus pumila, probably of named varieties. And in orchards? And with what other fruit? And with what uses?

And in Devon? The answer is surmise. Devon was a frontier district, with little evidence of farms or villas, so Malus pumila would have been rare if not unknown. Native Britons may have traded and introduced trees. The bigger question is whether apples, their cultivation (and therefore the potential for cider making) would have survived in England with the Roman Empire's collapse. Wildings perhaps, but the existence of orchards seems very unlikely.

Roman mosaic 'Autumn' of Pomona with pruning knife found under Dyer Street, Cirencester. (Corinium Museum, Cirencester)

Pears

We said above that orchard pears, Pyrus communis, also originated far away, in the Caucasus. They were known to the Romans who had named varieties, and so it is again probable that they introduced them to Britain. Wild pears found in Devon are not native: Pyrus pyraster was probably introduced from Europe by early settlers, while Pyrus cordata probably came from Brittany. Pyrus cordata is known as the Plymouth Pear, because it is known to grow near Plymouth as well as Truro. It would be nice to claim it as a Devon orchard fruit, but it is a plant of hedgerows with a tiny, rock-hard fruit. There was no case for growing it in an orchard.

Wilding apple tree at The Rings, north of Loddiswell.

Precautionary headgear when picking pears. Alex Hill makes Bollhayes Cider and Perry.

Plums

Plums are another fruit with exotic origins, indicated by the wide variety. In my garden near Barnstaple I have inherited three members of the family. Small, hard, black, bitter bullaces are considered by Harold Taylor to be the original wild plum (Taylor). There are sweet, red cherry plums taken by blackbirds, and Landkey Yellow plums that spread by suckering. The story is not simple, but is probably best understood by distinguishing between orchard fruits and those of hedgerows. Orchard plums, Prunus domestica, are thought to be the product of hybridisation between Prunus cerasifa and Prunus spinosa, probably in the Caucasus.

These parents have produced a great range of offspring from greengages and crimson Victorias to deep purple Marjorams. Hedgerow plums (damsons, bullaces, mirabelles and crislings) are Prunus institia. Routes to Devon have been various over a long period. Plums were grown at Glastonbury Abbey pre-Conquest, probably along with Devon monastic houses. Dittisham (near Dartmouth) has given its name to three varieties of plum; the short-seasoned but once-popular red, dessert Dittisham Ploughman is claimed to be the German Pflaummen Baum (plum); there are fanciful stories about its origin, but all agree that it was introduced.

Dittisham plums.

Collecting grafting material from ancient mazzard trees, Goodleigh.

Mazzards/Cherries

Growing in North Devon are trees and fruits known as mazzards – much diminished remnants of a much wider distribution. Their recent revival is described in Chapter 11. Mazzards are Prunus avium and therefore closely related to the wild cherries growing in Devon and across the country. There is North Devon folklore that the trees were introduced by Huguenots, but documentary evidence suggests earlier origins. So although the trees were certainly grown by later Huguenots, I surmise that the trees were domesticated from the wild. This could make mazzards the most 'native', the most 'Devon', of any fruit grown in the county's orchards. Ongoing genetic testing may prove me very wrong!

Cherries, cerises (as opposed to mazzards) had Norman origins, and Henry VIII's fruiterer, Richard Harris at his nursery at Teynsham in Kent, was very important for introducing continental varieties of Prunus cerasus.

So even if fruits have been introduced to Devon over a long period it does not mean they have been grown in orchards.

Ancient mazzard tree, Venn, Landkey.

Blossom at Compton Castle.
(Peter Rodd)

Ch 4
Medieval Decision Making

The origins of Devon's orchards is a matter not considered by many people, with a widespread assumption that there always must have been orchards around. We know that in medieval times fruit trees existed in Devon (although perhaps not many), but the existence of fruit trees does not mean that they were widely grown in orchards. Running a course called 'So you are thinking of planting an orchard?' I recall that most of the participants already owned an orchard and wanted to renew or extend it. Only a few had taken the brave decision to acquire land and plant an orchard from scratch. Some wanted to recreate orchards they had known as children. Others had been influenced by the campaign to prevent the disappearance of traditional orchards (and the grants that were sometimes available in support of the campaign). Certainly all the participants were carrying around concepts of orchards in their heads, and this was confirmed by a little exercise on what sort of orchard they wanted to create. But if you hadn't this concept in your head how would you grow fruit?

And it may have been late in Saxon historical times before many Devon people got the orchard concept in their heads. People would have grown and used fruit, but not in orchards as we know them. We've seen that word orchard originally meant something very different. We may never know when the salutation 'may their orchards be filled with apples/fruit (beop hyra orcerdas mid aepplum afyllede)' was first used in Devon. So how was fruit grown before orchards appeared on the scene?

The Romans grew grafted apples, and there is evidence in other counties of orchards around villas, such as Ditchley in Oxfordshire (Wright). Devon was never a county of villas, and so it will probably remain a mystery as to whether there were Roman orchards in the county, and whether there was any tradition of fruit growing maintained after the Romans' departure. There's a possibility that seedlings of Roman apples survived, even that there was grafting onto selected crabs, and that fruit trees featured in the rudimentary trade that persisted, but these post-Roman possibilities don't necessarily point to orchards.

Orchards are not the only way of growing fruit. Fruit trees in forests and woods would be known and spared the axe – a practice occasionally followed to this day. Mazzards, (wild cherries), were known for their timber and fruit, and the prized bowls and cups (masers) made from cherry wood could be used for collecting the fruit. However, most fruit trees only flourish in woodland glades or on woodland margins.

Cherry plum blossom, growing from suckers, Landkey.

25

HEDGEROW FRUITS

Hedges are such a common and characteristic feature of the English countryside that most people cannot envisage it without them. For some they are a 'natural' feature, but most are man-made. They can be very old and some in Devon may be as old as agriculture itself. In that sense there is a link with the 'natural' vegetation of the county.

Hedges are so old that the very word has evolved in meaning, and can mean different things in different places. *The New Naturalist* 'Hedges' has an opening chapter entitled 'What is a hedge?' (Pollard) It explains that our modern English word originates in the Anglo-Saxon word 'gehaeg' and that 'hay' and 'haw' originate from the same source. We still use 'haw' for hedge plants, and 'hay' meaning hedge is retained in some place-names. The hedge can be a stone or earth bank, a 'dead hedge' of dead vegetation, or a barrier of living vegetation.

The act of creating or managing a hedge usually involves planting, and this is dictated by function and plant availability. Early hedges may have been around woodland 'assarts', containing the wood and taking material from it. In other cases the function may be one of simple boundary demarcation, replacing 'perambulations' marked by solitary objects such as crab or scrub with a solid line of vegetation. Usually in Devon hedges are about animals – keeping them in or keeping them out. But these do not exclude the function of food production as a bi-product of the hedge itself. Plant availability in an age before decent transport or nurseries would depend initially on what was available locally. Harold Fox has suggested that the reason for enclosure may well have the incorporation of fruit trees (Fox).

So right from the start there would be crab apple, possibly 'wilding' apples, plum, cherry, wild pear and sloe. Even today there is a remarkable amount of recognisable and usable fruit in hedges. Evidence from Warwickshire suggests hedges could be described as the wild fruit habitat.

All fruit would be used and developed. In the thicket of the hedge (and hedges were thicker in the past, with trimmings left as a barrier), the trees would be safer from predators or stock.

APPLES While crabs have several uses, the main one is as a rootstock. Different varieties of Malus domestica could be grafted to them. In the course of time 'wildings', growing naturally from pips, would appear.

PLUMS There is a wide range. Bullace, sloe, damsons, cherry plums, and myrobalan plum are all found in other counties as well as Devon. But the sweet self-fertile crislin(g) seems localised in the the north: according to John Wright's English Dialect Dictionary the word 'chrisling' was mostly used in NW Devon.

CHERRIES Wild cherries are found in hedges, but height can make picking impracticable.

PEARS There are historic references to pears as boundary markers, so probably they were hedgerow trees. The Plymouth Pear may be found in hedges because of its hedging qualities rather than fruit.

Fruit trees would also be grown in hedges and hedge banks, and this practice could have been widespread. Medieval hedges were not the shrunken objects we see today, and we must envisage wider and more forbidding barriers as fields were hacked out of scrub or woodland. Trees could be shared: a grant by Aethelheard, king of Wessex in 739, lists four trees and one grove belonging to different owners on the boundary of an area of land (Hagen). Trees on boundaries were special and confirmed in boundary charters, where they were landmarks, and sometimes became place names, such as Perryhill Farm near Colyton. Who could forget a large pear tree in full blossom? The commonest variety might have been crab (Malus sylvestris), a non-gregarious tree, and more productive varieties (Malus pumila) could be grafted onto it, but its universality has been questioned (Juniper). Just as apple trees are found today along roads where fruit has been hurled, so there would have been 'wildings' (seedlings from pips which had grown up). Plums in many forms are found growing in hedges too, and there is early evidence of them being grafted onto sloes, with contemporary evidence from Glastonbury. This practice may have led to the survival of ancient varieties (Stocks). Thick hedges would, of course, protect young trees from damage by stock before the invention of wire netting guards. Harold Fox noted that tenants grew apple trees in their hedges, and says that it raises the interesting speculation that, in England at large, there is a connection between fruit growing and early enclosure (Fox). Many of the earliest estate maps, admittedly much later, feature trees in hedges; why are they there if not because of significance?

But I am rushing ahead. The Romans departed because of an inability to control huge population movements from the east. New peoples arrived and settled in Devon without familiarity with Roman agricultural practices. There have been lively debates about whether there was a dualistic system of 'old' and 'new' settlements, about the nature of early enclosure and the emergence of 'nucleated' villages. 'Even in Saxon times, however, beyond the compact villages and their open fields, and on across the "waste" of their outfields, one would have come across hundreds of small hamlets and of single farmsteads, each lying alone in a clearing of the oak and ash woods or upon the edge of the moorland' (Hoskins). Fruit growing in orchards in early Saxon times was highly unlikely; in the compact villages because of unfamiliarity and in small hamlets because of impracticality. Even by the ninth century, when Devon (Defenascir) had become part of the kingdom of Wessex, what we know about settlement, farming practices and diet is limited and controversial. On settlement and farming practices two centuries later Robert Higham goes back to the Domesday survey to deduce the most exact picture from contemporary sources. But there is slender evidence, such as place names, from England and Europe of fruit awareness and fruit growing (Roach); awareness was the protection of fruiting trees when forest was being enclosed.

So fruit would be collected from the woodland and its margins, and from the hedgerow. But where else? Admittedly many centuries later; the Exeter Diocesan Court records of tithe disputes relating to garden ground across the county has identified a repeated pattern of trees: apples, pears, plums and cherries, as revealed by Todd Gray. These were trees in garden ground, probably of different ages, and perhaps growing against and well protected by walls or buildings. In settlements with small populations and without the ability to keep, preserve or trade much fruit, and where modern day 'waste' of damaged fruit would be unknown, what would be the point of having many trees? (Cider may be the answer, and we'll come to that later.) So the numbers of trees might occasionally meet a definition of garden orchards, but there is no evidence of fields of trees of any magnitude. It is safe to presume that this was following a practice that had gone on for centuries. Producing vegetables and fruit must have been hard work, and it was probably largely the responsibility of women, aided no doubt by their children (Dyer).

If there were fruit trees in woods, hedges, around the houses, and in gardens, both planted individually or grafted on to existing stock, it is unlikely people would plant orchards from scratch, with very vague ideas about what they were creating. What might make them take the plunge? We need to know about land ownership, land management and decision-making in the rural economy of medieval Devon. In post-Conquest feudal England the King, bishops, nobles and monasteries all had big estates, and there was a manorial system that covered most of the rest. Estates were loosely federated land holdings with different complimentary roles assigned to them. There would obviously be variations according to size of estate, but they produced surpluses and generous keep for the household of the owner; it is unlikely that owners became involved in land use. Parallel with this must go an understanding of the market – how does a demand become established? Where demand for fruit was surplus to domestic needs, such as at big houses, monasteries, towns or where cider was made, there was a case for having more fruit trees. Following the Black Death there were big changes in agricultural practices and new opportunities were explored (Morgan). There were small orchards such as those leased in fifteenth century to a tenant at Aylesbeare 'to improve his tenure'. 'That their apples were destined for cider is clear from evidence relating to the "manorialization" of pressing: the fruit was taken to the lord's pound, and a small tax or payment in kind (equivalent to multure) exacted', says Harold Fox. At Bishop's Clyst in east Devon, in the late fourteenth century the manor gardens were neglected; only occasionally were apples, pears and cyder sold. Cider sold for a high price: 20s for two pipes in 1372 (Alcock). What if the farmstead garden was abandoned, and sheep had replaced vegetables, might sheep end up under the trees, particularly with Spring lambs?

Cider Measurements

Measures were only standardised in the nineteenth century, and are given here for a broad understanding of production:

Hogshead measures 54 gallons (quarter of a tun)

Pipe or butt equals half a tun (or 3 barrels) (108 gallons)

Tun is double the size of a butt and is equal to six barrels (216 gallons)

The continued growing of oats and rye right into Tudor times made Devon and Cornwall distinct (Fox). They had become entrenched in local diet, including drink. Ale made from oats was still popular locally in the sixteenth century; there are contemporary descriptions of mid-Devon's drink and its effect on strangers! (Hooker) Who drank the small amount of cider made? The question is raised because cider was rarely used instead of ale in gifts or in payments to

Dart bridge and blossom, Staverton. (Peter Rodd)

labourers; it seems not yet to have assumed its later place as a common item of diet. The Abbot of Tavistock had a cider press at Plymstock which the tenants used, paying toll in kind over the period 1392 to 1489, after which the orchard and press were farmed out for a yearly rent. In 1475 three pipes of new cider and three pipes of well-matured cider were shipped to the abbey for consumption there. But when it comes to expenditure on drink the Abbey's accounts are full of 'ale purchased' with no mention of cider (Finsberg).

So while for most Devonians in medieval times orchards and orchard fruits would be scarce there could be exceptions. The first was monastic houses, second were the manor houses, and third were boroughs and trading places.

Monastic Houses

To understand how monasteries might have been influential in the establishment of orchards one has to grasp their original nature. Let us be sceptical about statements such as 'The first orchards in Devon were planted by the Cistercians.' We know very little about the holy enclosures or monasteries of post-Roman or 'Celtic' origins, and they were so different from those that succeeded them that we can only guess about their horticultural practices but there were monastic communities working the land for their livelihood. St Augustine's official 'conversion' in the seventh century led to the gradual establishment of monastic house all over the country. Named orders (first the Benedictines), produced a more ordered and regulated system, with growing patronage after the Conquest. Essentially they were houses of prayer and worship, carried out by monks, supported by secular workers. Houses were large and small, rich and poor, but they all needed land, and the produce (or rents) from it, to ensure their survival. Patrons endowed monasteries with land; they usually provided the monastic site with lands around it. Land in other places was also given. Initially houses took a direct interest in their estates, but in the course of time this interest, particularly in respect of remote or outlying farms, became that of a landlord, with land tenanted on a rental basis. Monks were about prayer and worship, not experimental land management.

The first and key point is that monastic orders and houses were international. Quite a few houses, such as Modbury, Ipplepen, and Otterton (Avranches) were offshoots of continental ones. There would be monks, and sometimes heads of houses and their staff, who had been abroad and were familiar with continental practices. They would have relatively easy access to new farming techniques and became known for introducing them. Second, one of the ordered components of a monastic house was its infirmary with an associated sheltered herb garden for the production of drugs: fruit growing became an extension of this. Third, sheltered sites were often chosen, and a valley with water supply would be attractive. Whilst not defended, monastic houses were quite enclosed with lots of walls; they provided shelter for fruit growing. Fourth, endowed status enabled planting for the longer-term and on a larger scale. It is not difficult to conceive a monastery establishing a garden orchard beside its timeless grand new buildings.

But did they? The evidence is slight and hard to come by. There is no doubt that they worked to produced wine – the sacred drink for the Mass. However, monks lived by a rule which was pretty severe in terms of food and drink, generally followed even if sometimes exceeded. Fruit was a 'pittance', a small extra item made available on feasts and holy days. Torre Abbey had a fair-sized orchard to the north-east of the buildings. Finberg in his study of Tavistock Abbey shows that at Plymstock (on the Estate rather than beside the Abbey), the Abbot had a cider press worked by tenants, and paid for by a toll in kind. In 1475 four pipes of cider were brewed from the apples grown in the Abbot's orchard, and the tenants contributed three pipes by way of toll (Finberg). Another three, left over from the year before and now sufficiently matured, were shipped up the Tamar to Morwellham for consumption in the Abbey. A few years later the orchard and press were farmed out at a yearly rent of 26s8d. Disposal of monastic land at the time of the Suppression has shown that many house had orchards, usually linked to gardens. However, there is also plenty of evidence that monastic houses consumed and paid in ale in significant quantities, suggesting that while orchards and their products were known they did not have major significance.

So just because monasteries had orchards does not mean that they had a widespread influence on what was grown across Devon. At the Dissolution the King himself removed six loads of fruit trees from Chertsey monastery in Surrey to take to his newly acquired property of Oaklands. This indicates that well-nurtured monastic trees were precious and desirable, but it can also be seen as symbolic, of the breaking out to the secular world from the enclosed religious communities. Were monastic orchards rather like vineyards today? There, known-about, successful, but uncommon.

Manors

There is documentary evidence of early cider making (and therefore orchards rather than random fruit trees?) in South Devon. So, in 1285 at Exminster Manor thee was commercial cider making on quite a scale (Turner). In 1297 cider was made at Combe in Tynhyde, and in 1372 at Bishop's Clyst (Alcock). At Kerkenswell Manor 1452 there was pressing and purchasing. By the fifteenth century we have evidence at Cockington of the Lady of the Manor, Cristina Cary, in 1461 paying 7s5d 'to divers men and women for gathering apples; and 2s4d to one man watching the press and pressers at the time of making the said lady's cider' (Lang). Perhaps the pressers were paid in kind? More interestingly, as well as making cider she let her press, the pressers and the vessels thereto belonging for 16d. This suggests that while there was manoralisation of cider making, there were others with their own fruit who wanted to take advantage of her equipment. Still today it better for equipment to be shared than for small apple producers to go to the expense of providing their own. This does suggest quite a quantity of fruit. At the end of this period we get a picture of orchards as a discrete land use thanks to a thorough survey of the West Country Manors of Cecily, Marchioness of Dorset, Lady Harington and Bonwell in 1525. She owned properties nation-wide, but particularly in the West Country. In Devon they are across the county, but mostly in the south-east. Because of their location they can be taken as a random survey of orchard presence in non-monastic Devon at the time. The survey lists tenants and their land in terms of area, use and value; the uses are defined as arable, pasture, meadow, moor, hempland and orchards. Of the many tenancies there are only 27 mentions of orchards. And what is intriguing is that eighteen of them are located in just two manors, Bryxham [sic] and Woodford (Plympton St Mary). The first on the list for Bryxham is: 'Vincent Turpynean holds there one cottage with a garden and orchard adjoining containing one acre worth yearly 13/4d and pays yearly 6/8d.' This is pretty typical (although most are half an acre), suggesting a

Compton Castle, Marldon.

domestic orchard of fair size with cottage and garden nearby. The orchard is producing far more apples than any cottager could use, so what was done with the surplus? Cider is a safe presumption, and traded because Bryxham and Plympton are near the coast. The average rent for all land over all the manors is 8d per acre, and this figure is low because of a lot of inferior land, but one can nevertheless see why 6/8d for orchard land would be an attractive proposition to a landowner (Stoate).

Boroughs and Trading Places

Early markets must have been interesting phenomena. There was no infrastructure, they were just dates, days when people would gather and trade at an appointed place. But before long landowners were cashing in on the activity with charters and tolls. Towns were the best places for them, with artisans around to sell all manner of goods, and services for those attending. Towns as they grew themselves provided a market for rural produce, but towns remained small through the medieval period. Exeter was the exception. Fruits (and vegetables) are difficult to transport, so until modern times towns were surrounded by 'market' gardens which supplied the townspeople. The location of orchards which supplied Exeter and other towns is speculation. The profitable fifteenth century kersey trade led to an increase in imports to Exeter, and these included apples from Normandy, casting a question over local provision (Carus Wilson).

Cider travels better than ale or beer, so what was taken on vessels leaving Devon? Right back in the time of Henry II and the Crusades of Richard I the ports of Dartmouth and Plymouth were important, not only for conveying troops but also their stores (Stevens). In the Welsh Wars of 1277 and 1283 Totnes and Dartmouth provided store ships, and for Edward I's Gascony campaign in 1297 it was Plymouth. In 1302, to repress the rebellion of Robert de Bruce in Scotland, a fleet was assembled and the Prior of Plympton 'loaned' large of stores of wheat, malt, sheep and other provisions – so no evidence of orchard products, and malt suggests ale. 'During the reign of Edward III, the Black Prince assembled, in 1355, a force of 3000 and Devon, Cornwall and Somerset were scoured for wheat and wine', so again no mention of cider. Saltash's Charter of 1461 required ships and victuals (to include wheat, beans, peas, cheese, ale and bread) to be supplied for Western defence, but it was ale, not cider, that was listed. The transport of pilgrims to the shrine of Saint James at Santiago, from the fourteenth century, growing to well over a thousand annually, would mean quite a demand for drink, but again no evidence of cider.

By Tudor times there was a national fleet emerging, and with it more central control by the royal household. Plymouth became the major forward base of the Navy, and the Hawkins family dominated the victualling and storing of the fleet. 'There was always a high standard of victualling in Hawkins' ships and food supplied included live sheep and pigs (to provide fresh meat), plus apples and pears for the good health of his crews' (Stevens). There would probably be dried fruit too. By the time of Drake and the Armada there were over ten thousand sailors and troops to be fed and the amount of supplies required was substantial, with whole vessels used as victualling transports. That the apples and pears were grown locally seems reasonable speculation.

Conclusion

So here is an overview, a sort of snapshot, of Devon's orchards in medieval times. They would be rare. They would be extensions of gardens in monastic houses, and there may have been some in the gardens of the main houses. In gardens in towns, and in villages there would be small collections of fruit trees. The peasantry would collect fruit from trees around their houses and those nurtured in woods and hedgerows. Cider would be made, just as wine is made in Devon now, but it would be uncommon, (and controlled by the Monasteries or Lords of the Manor), and most people would drink watery ale. If this is right it rather stands on its head the image that orchards and cider drinking history has assumed in modern times. Orchards were not the culture of the common man, more their overlords. And small orchards might have been a feature of religious houses and trading places before they were seen widely seen in the countryside.

Dartmouth Community Orchard above the river. (P. Rodd)

Apple trees on ridges, Yelland Farm, Fremington. (Tim Potter)

Ch 5
Moving into the Modern Era

From the Black Death in the mid fourteenth century Devon's population grew very slowly until Tudor and Stuart times, reaching 227,157 by 1660 (out of an English total of just over 5 million) (Barry). Population in some villages might have remained lower than at the time of the Black Death, but towns, particularly Exeter, grew fast at the start of the modern era thanks to the woollen trade.

The modern era saw big changes. We will look at changes in diet, at the Court and great houses and then the common people: how fruit was eaten more, and particularly how Devon moved from a largely beer drinking county to one where cider was drunk everywhere. In the last chapter we have shown that religious houses had been the homes of gardens and orchards. In this chapter we will look at what we know about the Dissolution and orchards. We will then look at how farming practices changed in the modern era. We will look at two specific changes that had big effects on orchards: the growth of towns, and overseas trade.

But before that I should take you to Lyveden New Bield, a property of the National Trust in Northamptonshire which I visited in 2017. New Bield (New Building) was a garden lodge, perhaps best described as a vast folly, rich in Christian symbolism, built by Sir Thomas Tresham in Elizabethan times. Beside it he planted a massive orchard, and from letters to his workman a good picture emerges of what the orchard was like in terms of design and varieties, and these are guiding the National Trust in its re-establishment. But it is not like any other orchard that I have seen. For a start the orchard can be surveyed from a huge spiral mound which was constructed at one corner. It would have been a place of walks, picnics and relaxation amongst trees with religious symbolism. Sir Thomas Tresham and his buildings are nothing if not highly individual, and his orchard is too: a use of vast wealth to find a route to salvation. I am not wanting to suggest that Tresham's personal ideas necessarily carried much, if any, weight in Devon, but they do demonstrate that in Tudor times orchards had become things of great status and highly symbolic, and if we limit our approach to their functional utilitarianism we may be missing the point. And no greater confirmation of this can be that after Sir Thomas's death his widow sold a large number of trees to Robert Cecil, Secretary of State to the new King, James I.

Changes to Food and Drink

Henry VIII was impressed by the culture of the European courts, and his wife, Catherine of Aragon, had introduced a taste for fine fruit in the Tudor court (Thirsk). Courtly food in England at that time (particularly for men), was the food of the chase. Day after day men would hunt; game was safeguarded for them, and game was what they expected to eat, and cooked fruit could accompany it. Henry made changes. He promoted the cultivation of fruit trees and established a nursery at Teynham in Kent, run by Richard Harrys. We have mentioned that six loads of fruit trees from Chertsey Abbey were taken by the King. 'When vegetables and fruit ceased to be despised as the food of the poor, and became a fashionable food of the rich, a veritable revolution was slowly set in motion' (Thirsk). It's a long way from Kent to Devon, and it would be decades before Henry's encouragement of fruit growing had significant impact across the Devon landscape, but it would come. So through the Tudor era tastes changed, and probably at an accelerating pace. Certainly there was experimentation, with many different fruits grown. Products we hardly use today were important: an example is verjuice, a very acidic juice from crabs and apples, widely used in sauces.

Another major change was the move away from ale or small beer. There are numerous records throughout medieval Devon of ale, not cider, being used for gifts or payments. There was less barley than in other counties, but there were oats and rye, which had become entrenched in local diet, including drink. Ale made from oats was still popular locally in the sixteenth century, but Hooker, when surveying the county in Elizabethan times, claimed it was so foul that it made animals and men sick! It might gradually be replaced by ale made from barley, and later by beer with the arrival of hops, but it was not a leap to cider. Harvest fluctuations and the price of wheat in Exeter were studied some time ago, showing a gradual rise in grain prices throughout the sixteenth century (Hoskins and Beveridge). Beer making must have become more expensive. There were harvest fluctuations with a number of very bad grain harvests and shortages in the 1560s and late 1590s. If grain was in short supply and required for beer and bread was the price of beer pushed up, making cider a more attractive commercial proposition? Cider gradually became a commoner, better quality drink, requiring larger orchards, more expensive cider-making kit, and community involvement. Uffculme inventories made around 1600 have thirty references to cider and apples – quite outnumbered by sixty-eight to beer and beer making. It is the inventory of Richard Goodridge that gives us a full picture of what was going on. He is providing drink, both beer and cider, and the list is pure poetry, 'a tinning still, an apple chamber, four little barrels and three firkins, a great vat, a brewing vat and five little tubs, a brewing furnace and five buckets, two old barrels and two gibs, a malt house, two old tubs, hoops and vessel timber. A cider house, six pipes and three hogsheads, two vats, a malt hutch, and an orchard' (Stanes). A misinterpretation of Devon's historic household features could have led to an underestimation of the number of malting floors (and therefore the importance of beer making and drinking (Brears).

Ale was not a long-lasting drink and so was made in small batches at any time of year. It was seen as a domestic task, and for some women it was their year-round job. However, cider, like wine, had to be made at one season of the year and then stored; this required communal organisation and upfront investment both in terms of capital and revenue before there was a return. Apples have the disadvantage of seasonality ('bearing years' were noted with enthusiasm), but surplus can be stored as cider, and surplus encourages trading.

Monastic Dissolution and Orchards: a Stimulus
Monastic ownership and use of orchards on a large scale is challenged by data about the Dissolution. There is a misconception that monasteries were surrounded by their own estates, worked by the religious with some lay help. As we noted in the last chapter, most monastic lands (often scattered over a wide area, far distant from the monastery), had tenants who managed them, paying in service, kind or rent, (although by the time of Dissolution a simple rent was common). The Dissolution meant the monastic houses had new secular ownership; a new landlord to whom payment was made by the tenant. This means that while the 'religious' were dismissed or relocated those that had worked the land (and orchards) could presumably remain in place, or move. So the monastic gardeners, who knew about growing fruit, would be accessible to a wider world.

Just a few examples of orchard disposal are given here, thanks to Joyce Youings. John Ridgeway acquired Torre Abbey's Shiphay Grange 'cum omnibus messuagiis ortis pomariis, gardinis', also Elsham Grange and some of Buckfast's land. Richard Pollard's purchase of the Forde

Abbey estate included a grange with orchards, gardens and meadows. Sir Thomas Dennis acquired St Nicholas Priory, Exeter, with demesne and two mills as well as a farm with two and a half acres of orchard and garden – through marriage the Dennis lands became part of the Rolle Estate. Sir Richard Grenville's acquisition of Buckland Abbey included the farm of the site with orchards, gardens and meadows. The farm of the site of the tenements with orchards and gardens at Tunstall, Dartmouth went to George Rolle of Stevenstone and Nicholas Adams of Dartmouth. Joyce Youings notes that although the King's favourites like Lord John Russell did well, much of the land was bought by the old squirearchy or lawyers and civil servants. There was very little re-selling, so land was seen as a longer-term investment. She says that often those who 'did well' were families' younger sons 'of energy and talent' (Youings).

New Entrepreneurial Spirit

So how would a new landlord of energy and talent, protestant and entrepreneurial, change things? He would look at his orchard differently; he was aware of the new approach to food and drink, he would try and overcome any restrictive practices that previous owners had (for example relating to sales) and he would take advantage of new markets (we will show below what these were). To plant orchards on any scale was a big speculation, with money up front and no return for a number of years. It certainly didn't happen evenly across the county, and it certainly doesn't seem to have happened at once. In Tudor times there were considerable variations in the amount of other land available across the county. With a buoyant economy and land available there were new entrants: peasant farmers of the South Hams and artisans/tinners of the Teign Valley (Kew).

Writing his *Synopsis Chorographical of Devonshire* in Elizabethan times Hooker notes that Devonshire had 'orchardes and apple gardens'. Their three functions were: serving the needs of their own households, furnishing the market, and making 'syder'. The last of these three was profitable for those near the coasts in supplying shipping. It seems clear that what had started with Henry as a quest for fine dessert fruits had ended in Elizabeth's Devon with a big growth in cider production. Hooker's observations may be limited, but they introduce the concepts of trade and profit into fruit growing and cider making. This is no longer the fruits of monastery gardens or domestic activity but serious business.

So what is the other evidence? There is tantalising evidence from just a few big land owners of orchard planting and the pride that they took in this new activity. As Wyatt and Stanes say, 'For the husbandman with few resources innovation was a risk and it was often the gentry who introduced new crops or practices' (Wyatt). First there were lords of the manor; in total about 350. They were scattered over a large county, but in each part of it they would know each other and perhaps be intermarried. Second and third were ancient freeholders and leaseholders, (with three-life tenancies being introduced in Elizabethan times), who together became known as yeomen. They would be a member of a small coterie of landowners who would watch each other. Taking land out of production for a number of years before an orchard started fruiting, even with intercropping, must have seemed a risky venture. Five examples are given. At Dartington, as early as 1582, there was a new lease between owner, Gawen Champernowne, and yeoman John Edwardes of Deane Pryors; as well as a barn and poundhouse there was an orchard north of the parson's house. It was called a new Apple Garden, (interesting nomenclature – had it been called that already, or was it, in 1582, really new?) Already mentioned, Buckland Abbey in West Devon, a former monastic house, was later claimed to have the oldest orchard in Devon, planted around 1580, and its owner Sir Richard Grenville had also planted an orchard at Stowe, just across the Cornish border. Torre Abbey in South Devon had similar origins and retained its orchards and provides an early

Apple tree on ridge and surrounded by way muck, Yelland Farm, Fremington. (Tim Potter)

contemporary illustration. Admittedly later (1644), the Earl of Bath's orchard was at Tawstock Court near Barnstaple in North Devon.

It is hard to know how quickly this new idea of planting orchards spread. At Shapwick in Somerset, a village in which Glastonbury Abbey's curia produced c1000 apples each year from their great garden, a multidisciplinary project has investigated the history of the village over millennia. Documentary references to orchards have been supported by archaeologically revealed tree holes, definitely post-Reformation, which suggests there was a widespread laying down of gardens and orchards after the Dissolution (Aston) But at Uffculme in 1604 John Chick, aged 77, said that there were 'very few apple orchards in the parish when he first new [sic] it'. He was answering questions on the tithe (Stanes). In the 1811 edition of Tristram Risdon it is noted that cider has long held a distinguished place in the rural economy. It records that in 1630 it was being produced 'in such plenty 'as many copyholders pay their Lord's rent with their cyder only'.

So how did this 'laying down' take place? Fruit trees require protection in an enclosed space. Were trees planted in existing enclosures, or were new enclosures established? It seems that many orchards when first mentioned are small; some are called apple gardens and many are associated with gardens. Orchards we describe as 'traditional' often have more than one function; in the past crops were grown between the trees. There is evidence from Dunsford as early as 1539 of a hay crop being taken. A messuagege called Halstone had a garden and an orchard (named Blewneorchard), and the hay was stored in a barn with just three horses. Orchards often doubled as 'mowbartons' or rickyards – trees providing shelter for the ricks. Sometimes tree spacing allowed for cash crops between the trees. And it is still usual for orchards beside farms to be used as shelter at lambing time, or for calving, or for sick animals. Did this practice start in Tudor times?

Stimulus: the Growth of Devon's Towns

From medieval times there had been a tradition of hucksters and victuallers coming to towns, particularly Exeter, with fruit and vegetables from quite far away, and even imported from Normandy. Because fruit selling was largely women's work and unprofitable it has been undocumented (Kowaleski). There would have been gardens, and perhaps small orchards producing apples, pears and plums in and around the towns, and more money to purchase thanks to the prosperity of the woollen cloth trade in Tiverton, Cullompton, Exeter and other places. However, the first map of Exeter (Hooker, 1587), shows gardens but no obvious orchards within the walls or outside; the tenter grounds for stretching cloth are there, but no orchards. Over a century later the maps show a different story.

Within the towns there was a lot of small-scale domestic brewing, again women's work. An early Tudor case before the Mayor's Court at Dartmouth accused the brewers of Stoke Fleming of bringing apple beer (cider) into the town (Watkin); ale and imported wine were the drinks of the town, not cider, and there were protective systems to ensure this remained the case. The later introduction of beer enabled larger units of production because the preservative effect of hops enabled it to be kept longer, and old maps occasionally show hop gardens where orchards might be expected.

The southern ports of Devon would have enabled the export of cider (and fruit) to the lucrative market of London. Kent was better placed for fruit, and Herefordshire lacked easy access to the coast for shipping, so cider was traded from Devon.

Stimulus of a Maritime Market

Devon's proximity to the sea and maritime activity has had a big influence on orchards, albeit an unobvious one. We are talking about the victualling needs of different maritime activities. First, there were the occasional demands of

THE DEVON ORCHARDS BOOK

overseas military ventures, and later the Navy. Second there was the age of maritime exploration. Third came overseas settlements, preceded by the exploitation of overseas resources, particularly fish.

Maritime Exploration

Writing in 1549 John Coke cites a debate between the Heralds of England and France (probably propaganda), saying that England is endowed with fruits, and so plentiful with peres and apples, 'that in the weste partes of England and Sussex they make perry and sydre, and in such abundance that they convey a part over the sea.'

Who claimed of writings on the Tudor Period that there are about three lines on the discovery of North America and a hundred pages devoted to Anne Boleyn? There was of course in Tudor times an overlap between defending the realm, privateering and discovering new lands. In many cases they involved the same ships and the same men. But exploration required longer journeys, and victualling was critical. 'In the last expedition of Drake and Hawkins to the West Indies in 1595, the ships were manned, armed and victualled at local charge with the Devon towns of Dartmouth, Plymouth, Totnes, Barnstaple and Exeter contributing. The victualling arrangements were planned by Sir John Hawkins who undoubtedly paid more care and attention to these matters than any other sea captain in the Elizabethan era' (Stevens). The importance of cider and apples on long sea voyages has been overlooked in the past and deserves more attention – and apples and pears (in barrels) too (Crowden). There are three destinations that had strong links with Devon. First, Newfoundland. Second what was termed 'southern climes' with Barbados being a very important destination: 'The merchants who make great voyages to sea, find it a very useful drink in their ships and so buy up a great store of it, for one ton of cider will go as far as three of beer and is found more wholesome in hot climates' (K C Turner). Third, North America: the Pilgrim Fathers took cider with them.

What did they drink? Memorial to Devon's Newfoundland fishermen, Bideford.

All these supplies could not have been produced without an impact on the local economy. It would be simplest for victuallers to go to the bigger suppliers, and to use cash or credit rather than exchange, so this would encourage speculation and investment. Investment in orchards does not produce results overnight. For the earliest voyages in Elizabethan times cider and fruit in small quantities could be drawn from existing orchards. As demand increased in to the seventeenth century there must have been an increase in the number of orchards, probably over the hinterlands of Plymouth, Dartmouth, Teignmouth, Exmouth and Bideford/Barnstaple – perhaps not Exeter which seems to have been conservative in terms of investment in longer voyages. Prevailing transport problems would rule out most inland areas. But could maritime demands have raised cider in Devon's consciousness, and stimulated orchard planting across the county for other reasons?

Marion Hardy shows that in the case of Newfoundland victualling of fishing vessels developed into a permanent trade. 'As early as 1622, Devonian Whitbourne's list of victuals for a ship to undertake a voyage to Newfoundland included "26 tun of beere and Sider" at 53s4d per tun (Hardy). Francis Bacon says cider was taken to Newfoundland from Exmouth as an ant-scurvy measure, because early French explorers were decimated. Nobody was sure what prevented the disease. Modern factory-made ciders contain little of the Vitamin C which prevents scurvy, but maybe older production methods had more. Early on there was no permanent settlement on Newfoundland, so how did the fishermen survive? Probably they lived on fish, but what did they drink? Two centuries later when Newfoundland had a permanent population, about a third of them from Devon, merchant William Codner of the Teign estuary, advertised for sale in St John's exported 'Prime Devonshire Ale and Cider'. One notes that in both victualling and trade it is beer that is listed before cider.

Stimulus: Publications and Know-How

The early modern period is the first age in western civilisation with printed books, and in the native language. So we find in the seventeenth century a huge blossoming of publications advocating good practice in orchard management, tree varieties and cider production. Some of the best known are listed, and they would have been known by the best landowners of the county; I have indicated the areas from which the writers derived their expertise. How much significance should we attach to the absence of texts based on Devon experience? It cannot have helped raising the standards of fruit growing or cider making that we have to wait until the eighteenth century for writers like Hugh Stafford of Pynes near Exeter. When Celia Fiennes travelled in the South West she made no observations on Devon's orchards or cider, but was critical of standards in Somerset, another county without specific publications. Andro Linklater, emphasising the sheer speed of change quotes the poet George Puttenham (1589) complaining of the experiments that made 'the white rose redde, yellow or carnation, a bitter melon sweete, or sweete apple soure, a plumme or cherrie without a stone, a peare without core or kernell…' Experimentation encouraged the growing of fruit, and Gerard's Herbal (1597) lists many new varieties, so that in 1629 Parkinson said that it was impossible to list all the varieties grown. So this was 'improvement', and recent experience shows that the ready availability of interesting varieties is an incentive to plant. Nationally, the Livery Companies of Fruiterers and Gardeners date from 1605.

Conclusion: What Were Orchards Like

Studying contemporary sources reveals a lot of commonplace rather than specialised information, suggesting that many contemporary readers had a lot to learn about orchards, fruit and cider. Many stress the wide range of uses for fruit. For example, John Parkinson in his *Paradisi in Sole Paradisus Terrestris* 1629 says of apples: 'The best sorts…serve as the last course for the table, in most men's houses of account; where if there grow any rare or excellent fruit, it is then set forth to be seene and tasted. Divers other sorts serve either to bake, either for the Master's Table or the meynes sustenance, either in pyes or

Advice for Orchard Owners (Seventeenth and Eighteenth Centuries)

Anon: 1 *'A Lover of Planting' The Compleat Planter and Ciderist* (1685) (Note: Mentioned by Sir Roper Lethbridge)
2 *Treatise on Cider* (1678)

Ralph Austen (1612-76) (Staffordshire and Oxford) *Treatise of Fruit Trees and The Spiritual Use of an Orchard* (1653)

John Beale (1608-1683) *Herefordshire Orchards: a Pattern for all England* (1656 or 1657?)

John Evelyn (1620-1706) (Surrey and London) *Sylva-Pomona* (1664)

John Evelyn's book on fruit trees (1670)

Thomas Andrew Knight (1759-1838) *Treatise on Culture of Apple and Pear and Manufacture of Cider and Perry* (1797), and also *Pomona Herefordiensis* 1808-1811

Batty Langley (1696-1751) *Pomona or Fruit Garden Illustrated*, (?1729), contains a contribution by Hugh Stafford on Devon cider fruit. (Note: Owned by Eric Whiteway, and copy in Whimple Heritage Centre).

William Lawson *A New Orchard and Garden* (1631)

Captain Gervaise Markham *The Whole Art of Husbandry*, (second book). *Of Gardens, Orchards and Woods* (1631) (Note: Mentioned by Sir Roper Lethbridge)

Leonard Mascall (1572-1656) (Bucks) *Book of the Arte of and manner howe to plant and graffe all sotes of trees, how to set stones, and sowe Pepines to make wylde trees to graffe on.*

John Rea (d1685) ((Shropshire) *Flora, Ceres and Pomona* (1665)

H. Stafford *A Treatise on Cyder Making* (1759) (also see Batty Langley) (Note: In Devon&Exeter Institution Library)

John Worlidge (1640-1700) (Hampshire) *Vinetum Britannicum or a Discourse on Cider* (Note: Was owned by Richard Coffin of Portledge, also mentioned by Sir Roper Lethbridge)

---

pans, or else stewed in dishes with Rosewater and Sugar and Cineman or Ginger cast upon. Some kinds are fittest to roast in the winter time, to warm a cup of wine, ale or beere, or to be eaten alone, for the nature of some fruit is never so good or worth the eating, as when they are roasted. Some sorts are fitted to scald for codlins and are taken to coole the stomach… It is usually seen that those fruits that are neither fit to eate raw, roasted or baked, are fittest for cider and make the best. The juice of Apples… is of very good use in Melancholic diseases, helping to produce mirth and expel heaviness. The distilled water of the same apples is of like effect'. When John Vowell (1524-1601) wrote his *Hooker's*

MOVING INTO THE MODERN ERA

Synopsis Chorographical of Devon, (Hooker was Vowell's nom de plume) in the 1590s it remained in manuscript. It is mostly about antiquarian interests, but the volume starts with a useful account of the agriculture of the county. He says about Devon, 'They have also orchards and apple gardens which be stored with all kindes of good frutes and those in the tymes of the yere they do dresse prune and trymme by opening the rootes, by paringe away the waterie howes and by graffinge of theym by which meanes they be made very frutefull…' There is the first significant list of fruit varieties: 'for frute trees great changes as the aple and peares wch in the pticulers be hardly to be named but yet of many theise few be most in use, as of aples the pepyn the renate Cowicke quarenden, Comewater, pomewater, bellebone, portegue, Tretegolde Churnpayne the soure aple the sweete aple the Crabbe tree the syder frute. And of peares the Sowton peare the peare mayne the bishops peare the Genet ['the Kathergt peare' crossed through] the Grace peare the warden and many others not to be named.'

And, of course, we would like to know so much more about these late Elizabethan orchards; so many questions are begged. If the orchards had all kinds of fruits (thirteen are listed, according to Daniel Lysons), this meant special protection, probably walls. It was said that Grenville's orchard at Buckland Abbey was the oldest in Devon (by William Marshall in 1796!), because there is much evidence of small orchards from earlier times. 'According to Mr Stapleton of Monk's Buckland, orchards in the district started at Buckland Priory around 1596, and orchards are still there, and bearing well'. In 1626 Sir Bevill Grenville implored his wife to protect his precious fruit trees (at Stowe, near Kilkhampton across the Cornish border, and no longer there) from marauding animals by filling hedge gaps. So this fruit was in an enclosure that was hedged, not in a walled garden. In 1591 a Pear Garden was planted at West Ogwell, to be followed by an apple orchard in 1597 (Gray, *Devon Gardens*). In 1644, Henry, 5th Earl of Bath, had a new 2-3 acre orchard planted at Tawstock, near Barnstaple, where he lived. It was designed in four quarters, and there were 268 trees: apples, pears, quinces and damsons. Also he built a 'fair wall about it, slated and tiled' presumably cob, and this was planted with apricots, peaches, cherries and nectarines. This was 1645, when the Civil War, was raging! However, Todd Gray's analysis of the Earl of Bath accounts show that beer was a significant item in the household, but not cider. However, ten years after the orchard was planted, (the usual time for standard trees to come into significant bearing), the Accounts are recording income from seams of apples and hogsheads of cider (Gray).

Log pile and young trees in standard orchard at Bradford Barton. (Tim Potter)

An orchard at Shute today.

Ch 6
Devon Orchards and the Cider Explosion

Context

In Tudor times landowners looked for alternatives to grain and livestock. In Devon they had seen an alternative as orchards, and taken to them in a widespread way, and by the mid seventeenth century they were no longer 'alternative' but becoming 'mainstream'. So orchards were established at big houses such as Buckland, Tawstock and Shute. Shute was big money, with expensive surrounding walls, trees brought in from London and dedicated staff. And at unremarkable villages like Uffculme, where there had not been orchards before, there were new ones, and cider making equipment stood alongside beer making kit. Orchards were becoming a familiar and fast-expanding feature in the Devon landscape.

We have shown what brought this change about. Then, in the seventeenth century, this significant change became something even bigger. Many Devonians were urged on by the expanding literature on the best fruit varieties and orchard management practices (Box in Chapter Five). This media frenzy took me back to my youth when I enjoyed reading Alexander Dumas's *The Black Tulip*. It was about the tulip mania in seventeenth century Holland, and how spare cash and desire for profit can lead staid horti-culturalists to speculate. I have recalled that book: 'bubble' might be the word, but growing trees and fruit and making cider became part of a sort of horticultural zeitgeist. Both the big house and the ordinary man were all joined in a big change. 'Apples became a national fruit, and cider was the patriotic tipple, believed to be able to nourish the nation, establish the Empire and win Wars' according to Claire Preston. Ralph Austen had even argued the case (to Cromwell) that planting orchards was a Protestant duty.

So trees and orchards and cider drinking were part of a new national consciousness, driving up standards and leading to experimentation. Strong bottles, and secondary fermentation is another story. Foreign wars limited the import of wine and cider replaced it – sometimes with confusing nomenclature. A contemporary traveller, Daniel Defoe, wrote about the mixing of cider (not specifically from Devon), with wine by the London vintners. This form of discrete adulteration would certainly not have been advertised, so we have little idea as to its scale and whether in any sense it increased demand and therefore may have underpinned orchard planting.

In 1657 John Beale wrote about Herefordshire orchards, 'One reason why fruit do so abound in this Country, is for that no Man hath of late years built him a House, but with special regard to the proximity of some Ground fit for an Orchard. And many times, Servants when they betake to Marriage, seek out an Acre or two of Ground which they find fit for Orchards: for thus they give a Fine, or double value for years of Lives; and thereon they build a Cottage, and plant an Orchard, which is all the Wealth they have for themselves and their Posterity'. An orchard could be seen as both security and speculation: for little labour there was usually a return, and in some years a very good one.

The Devon Picture

Thomas Westcote's *A view of Devonshire in DCXXX* (1630) probably drew on Hooker's work, (see Chapter Five), but there are subtle differences. He says 'They have of

SHUTE AND SIR COURTENAY POLE

Shute, now known as Shute Barton, near Colyton, has been described as a 'trophy house'. What stands today are the domestic quarters of a much grander mansion which was largely demolished in the Eighteenth Century and replaced by nearby Shute House.

This material is drawn from Todd Gray in *Devon Gardens*.

The old house was acquired by the Pole family from nearby Colcombe in the seventeenth century. Sir Courtenay Pole, known in parliament as Chimney Pole because of his enthusiasm for the Hearth Tax (remarkable because Shute had 29 hearths!), is a significant figure in the development of Devon orchards. First he planted a huge number of trees. Second his accounts show records of his purchases and show that he was introducing varieties from other parts of the country as well as from local sources. Third there are named varieties of apple. Fourth he had his own nursery (at Colcombe). Fifth he seems to have delighted in the practice of grafting.

In 1658 he acquired trees from Captain Slade of Axminster, and also had grafting material from a family house at Bromley-St-Leonards (near Stratford in east London) where his father died the same year. In 1660 he paid £4.5s for 32 different fruit trees from London (and there were possibly more), and we know many of the varieties (see below). In 1663 he had 144 'fair handsome trees' from his cousin Nathaniel Pole at Escot, and at the same time 64 from John Wickes of Larkbeare in Talaton. At about the same time 67 pear trees were acquired from the son of John Pincent, the former Rector of Talaton, and nine years later they hadn't produced much fruit. Was the expression 'pears for heirs' not known to him? 1668 saw him noting the planting of two hundred Gillyflower (apple) trees. In 1669 he had plum and apricot trees sent down from London, and the same year acquired apple, medlar and French walnut. In 1671 he bought 30 young apple trees from the son of 'old Mr Paulmer'. And, of course, there were trees from his own nursery – perhaps the Gillyflowers of 1668?

Of the named varieties of apple the 'Gersie' of 1658 was very red both within and without – this was from Captain Slade of Axminster. The grafts from Bromley-St-Leonards were Spanish Pippin, Russetting, Old Wife, Golden Rennett, Apple Dainty, Codling, Gillyflower and the Summer Apple. In 1663 those from Nathaniel Pole included French Long Stay. Of the varieties he brought down from London in 1660 he recorded apricots (some of which were an early variety), pears (both Bergamot and summer Chretien), peaches (Newington, Nutmeg, Double Blossom and Carnation), nectarines (Roman, Red and Green), plums (Queen Mother and Grass), cherries (Duke and May) and three 'malligottoones' presumably melocoton (which was a peach grafted onto a quince stock).

Todd Gray gives no information on the nursery at Colcombe, nor the rootstocks on which the trees were grown. An illustration shows espaliered trees against a wall (peaches and nectarines could hardly have been grown otherwise), and in 1658 a lot of bricks were acquired (for a garden wall?). There is a suggestion that there was a kitchen garden as well as a walled garden. The grafts from Bromley-St-Leonards were grafted onto trees in the Great Orchard, set out in at least twelve rows with up to fourteen trees per row. Does the name Great Orchard suggest very much larger trees than those in the walled garden? The trees from cousin Nathaniel at Escot were brought with eight horses which suggests trees of some size destined for an orchard and not a garden.

Dates of grafting are given as 7 and 8 April. He conducted an experiment with grafting more than one variety on to the same tree.

late years much enlarged their orchards, and are very curious in planting and grafting all kinds of fruits, for all seasons, of which they make good use and profit, both for furnishing their own table as furnishing of the neighbour markets… But most especially for making of cider, a drink both pleasant and healthy; much desired of seamen for long southern voyages, as more fit to make beverage than beer, and much cheaper and easier to be had than wine.' Enlargement and curiosity: Westcote's description of cider as 'a drink both pleasant and healthy' suggests promotional advertising language to those who are unfamiliar with it. Would he have needed to describe beer in such a way? (Westcote)

Elsewhere Westcote's book talks of the great variety of fruits in Devon. 'We are also furnished with great variety of fruits, and most of them sundry choice of species.' He suggests 'fruitful trees' border the meadows and marshes – a rather different picture than in the cottagers' gardens or around the larger towns. Certain places, such as Ermington (South Hams) and Goodley (sic, North Devon), are described as fruitful (the latter for its mazzards). Places don't just become fruitful; they become so because people have planted trees, and nurtured those trees into fruitfulness, a process of decades. Those trees had probably been planted in the reign of Elizabeth. But he also notes certain places like Modbury (South Hams, not far from Ermington) and Braunton (North Devon, not far from Goodleigh) are renowned for their beer, so Devon is still not wholly a cider county!

The Royal Society set up its Georgicall Committee in 1664 to examine the state of agriculture in the country. Devon was one of the few counties to respond thanks to the efforts of Samuel Colepresse. Livestock and grain are the pre-occupation, reflecting the interests of national 'improvers', and he doesn't pick up orchards as part of this.

For a contemporary Devon picture we have to wait until Hugh Stafford of Pynes near Exeter wrote enthusiastically about his county in a 'Letter to a Friend' dated 1727 (Stafford). This 'friend' was in fact Batty Langley, a nurseryman of Twickenham, who included the letter in his own *Pomona*, published in 1729. Stafford says 'It is a maxim. which merits observance, that in planting an orchard, the several excellences of the kinds intended for that purpose should be previously well considered, whether they are such as are inclined to make large, lasting and kindly trees, fruitful and hardy, and not subject to blights, which frequently make them miscarry in their bearing, that the fruit they produce make the best cider, and that all kinds may ripen about the same time, or at two or three several times, in quantities of each sort sufficient to make a tunning at one time; which last properties are of no small consideration for the more regular and commodious making of cider'. Much of his account is about apple varieties and the origin of the Royal Wilding – an apple of 'body, roughness and flavour' which cider drinkers in Devon desire. Other varieties are listed, but few from Devon. On planting he says that it is impossible to prescribe spacing because of the variability of conditions (such as soil, aspect, exposure). He also suggests that Devon growers had not mastered rootstocks, for he says 'and as the growths of trees are so unlike one another, some inclining to a pyramidal or conic form, others to spread, and some in the best situation or soil become but mere shrubs or bushes, whilst some acquire the bulk or stature of Oaks… so without being acquainted with the growth of each particular kind, no rules can be formed' Red-streaks took less than half the space of Midyates and White-sours.

Milles Survey

We have the first comprehensive picture of orchards across the county of Devon thanks to a remarkable survey undertaken from 1747 by Jeremiah Milles.

To the question 'What quantity of acres under Orchards?' 79 respondents (from 258 parishes) didn't know, two said there were none, 124 gave acreages, 15 said they had many, with unknown acreages, and 32 said they had few– again with acreage unknown. A few of the 79 quoted

> ## DEAN MILLES'S SURVEY
>
> Jeremiah Milles (1714-1784) conducted a parochial questionnaire survey of the Exeter diocese when a prebendary, prior to becoming Dean of Exeter. In 1757 printed questionnaires were sent to the incumbents of 461 parishes. There were 120 questions in total, with some on the current economy including orchards and cider production. His circulated questionnaire is seen as pioneering this research technique. 263 returns (57%) were received. Like many such surveys today the results were never analysed or printed! The returns reside in Oxford's Bodleian Library, with a microfiche with the South West Heritage Trust in Exeter.
>
> The five questions relating to orchards and cider were:
> What quantity of acres under Orchards?
> What sort of Apples are planted, or are found to agree best with the soil?
> What quantity of Cider is generally made yearly?
> Is it remarkable for its goodness? Is it of the rough or sweet sort?
> And what is the usual value of it per hogshead at the Pound's mouth?
>
> Of the 263 returns a handful were not worth analysing, but 258 were transcribed into printed form by Sir Roper Lethbridge and published in the *Transactions of the Devonshire Association* in 1900 (Lethbridge). The responses for the 258 parishes are variable. A few incumbents objected, for example the orchard questions for West Worlington were erased, while the respondent for Brendon said there was just one acre of orchard in the parish 'which I desire you'll come and measure'. But on the whole incumbents co-operated, and in some cases sought assistance – on cider production at Culmstock 'the question was put to the Exciseman but he could not answer it'. If not sure of the answers they leave it blank or write such as 'I know not' or 'Nescio'. In a very few cases the writing is illegible.
>
> There is no doubt that orchards and cider were very significant aspects of Devon's rural economy in 1757, and thank you Dean Milles for recognising this.

tenancy arrangements such as Feniton where 'Every cottage has some Apple Trees. An Estate of £40 a Year an Acre or upwards' – but what is that in acreage? Barnstaple, Goodleigh, Landkey, Swimbridge noted their totals included mazzards, and Bere Ferrers included cherries. The parish with the biggest acreage emerged as Paignton with 300 acres. The following had 150 acres or more: Brixham, Buckland Monachorum, Fremington, Lankey [sic], St Marychurch, Milton Abbot, Plimtree, Staverton, Shobrook, Swymbridge (sic), Tavistock, Tawstock, Tawton Bishop (sic) and Upottery. By totalling the acreages given (7444), and guesstimating 'many' orchards as meaning 100 acres/parish and 'few' as 20 acres/parish, we arrive at just over 9000 acres of orchards for 179 respondents to this particular question. This amounts to just about 50 acres per parish, which would total at 23,000 acres for the whole of Devon. This is less than a third of the acreage recorded in the Tithe Survey a century later. The precise acreages for Northam and Ottery St Mary were not given because new planting was going on, so was considerable planting ongoing? Or could Milles's correspondents be underestimating?

Another approach is looking at cider production. Stanes used Milles's figures to say that by 1750 Devon's annual production probably totalled 170,000 hogsheads or 10 million gallons. This would mean about 7 hogsheads per acre for the acreage given in the last paragraph. This seems high, suggesting Milles's respondents underestimated orchard acreages. Assuming Devon's population in 1747 was 300,000 this means 33 gallons/head. Admittedly much cider was exported, but Stanes has the throw-away line that beer was

EIGHTEENTH CENTURY APPLE VARIETIES

So what varieties were grown? John Worlidge (1691) produces a national list with geographical origin. Varieties attributed to Devon include Bitter Scale, Dean's Apple, Deux Ans, Devonshire Quarrington, Kirton Pippin, Marigold (or Pleasantine) and Oaken Pin. What is signified by Hugh Stafford's (1753) omission of most of them in favour of Cockagee, MidYate (or Mediate), Royal Wilding and White Sour?

The Milles returns are interesting because they are for each parish. Admittedly about 180 of the Milles respondents faltered answering this technical question, with blanks or replies like 'No particular' or 'Very Few'. About 60 respondents named about 66 sorts or varieties. The Sandford reply 'Duzans' I originally took to mean 'Dozens of varieties' before tumbling to 'Deux Ans'. Nearly all apples listed are cider apples, with a few like Golden Pippin, Golden Russet, Marigold and Pearmains being thought suitable as table fruit too. St Budeaux near Devonport and Plymouth, and Newton Ferrers upstream, grew 'all table fruits' as well as cider apples. Townstall grew all sorts, but hardly any table fruit, while Bridgerule was able to grow table fruit because it was sheltered. Paignton had 'hoard fruits' which could be used for cider. Of the cider apples listed some are surely 'sorts' rather than varieties. Bittersweets are mentioned by 15 and Wildings by four (but what are Royal Wildings mentioned by 12?). The respondent for Feniton says they grow 'South Ham fruits viz White Sour, Baccamore, Kerling and Royal Wilding', and five other respondents list Southam [sic] fruits without spelling out which. White Sour gets 26 mentions, Mediates 24 and Baccamore 17, with Redstreaks getting 12. Colebrookes plus Red, White and Royal Colebrookes total 14. No other varieties get more than five mentions, and 23 get only one. Surely the respondent from East Allington hit the nail on the head with 'Colebrookes, Bittersweets, Mediates, Oaken Pins and divers others called by names hardly known or heard of at 2 miles distant'. Changes are noted by a few: at Modbury White Sours are being supplanted by Baccamores, Colebrookes and Redstreaks, while at Rose Ash Royal Wildings and Golden Rennets are being introduced to meliorate the cider.

John Bury DL from Braunton kindly showed me a diary for 1787 that had belonged to his wife's ancestors. Inside the front cover is a list of newly acquired apple trees and where they were planted. Only 10% (Tom Putt, Lucombe and Broad-eyed [Kirton] Pippin) are Devon apples; most of the rest (including Yellow Styre, Red Styre, Cowarne's Red, Ten Commandments and Foxwhelp) are from Herefordshire. The diary also recorded income – from cider and, unexpectedly, dried apples.

An early record of plantings at Buckland Manor, Braunton.

Francis Hancock (left) with Apple Store at Harford Barton, Landkey. (Tim Potter)

also drunk. Devon had indeed become a cider county!

Milles's survey picks up the huge interest in varieties, and finding are summarised in the Box on page 46. Many varietal names varied from parish to parish, but it is clear from other sources that top grafting with nationally acclaimed varieties was becoming commoner. Lucombe's was established by 1720 as an Exeter nursery, but the name doesn't appear.

There seems to be only an awakening awareness of the importance of soils. Lethbridge says 'One point brought out very plainly is that various soils are suited to various sorts of apples, and that no general rule holds'. For instance, the Vicar of Feniton says that 'the redder the land the better the cider,' whereas in Harpford parish we are told that the apples thrive 'better in the clay than in the sand'. And in Hatherleigh the vicar states, 'All agree, except Redstrakes, which canker to nothing in all parts, and Shilson Pippins, which canker always in ye red, but thrive well in ye brown land.' The combination of soils and climate could explain why, according to respondents, making good cider was more an uphill task in northern parts. Milles does not ask for information on orchard cultivation. There is only the occasional mention of table fruit.

The survey shows clearly that some parishes were making good cider in large quantities and earning considerable money in the process. West Ogwell's was 'remarkably good', Gittisham's was a 'good masculine cider'

DEVON ORCHARDS AND THE CIDER EXPLOSION

community that was used to foul beer might accept pretty foul cider? Many parishes were more than self-sufficient and were able to benefit from trading. Brian Short notes from records of Duke of Richmond's Goodwood Estate that in March 1747 19 shillings was paid for freight and wharfage relating to two hogsheads of cider which had been sent via Exeter.

Mazzards

So far our tale has been all about apples. They completely dominated the planting that went on, although there would have been the tiny proportion of pears, plums and cherries. An exception is the mazzard, a form of cherry grown in North Devon to the east of Barnstaple. Its origins are obscure, and I take the view that it could have been naturalised from the wild cherry. There must have been significant early 'gardens' (that is the term used), because the fruit was served at Tawstock Court in the 1640s and featured in 'feasts' at Goodleigh. Why would people in an area of low population and poor access to significant markets plant large areas of a very perishable fruit? There is no doubt that the fruit is delicious, and that would make it very special when palates had not tried many of the exotic fruits accepted as commonplace today. Would owning a mazzard orchard bring prestige to its owner? And at a time of wealth in Barnstaple could the mazzard have been a subject of speculation?

Towards a War and a New Century

We have to wait until the turn of the century before contemporary agricultural commentators produce an update since the time of Milles. Two interesting orchard-related issues, Cider Tax and Devonshire Colic, are described in Boxes. Both point to how significant Devon's orchards had become. Indeed, the Cider County's orchards can be seen to have their modest place in history in these two respects. First, the debate about the Excise tax and

Door frame altered to accommodate barrels, Harford Barton, Landkey. (Tim Potter)

and Ottery St Mary's was a 'good, racy cider, improving annually'. There were some makers, such as at Staverton who paid attention to making a good drink, but many didn't. Lethbridge says that the Milles survey corroborates what Hugh Stafford had said in his letter of 1727 and book of 1753 'in every detail. The quality of the cider differed immensely in different parishes, owing probably as much to errors in cultivation or making as to differences of soil and aspect' (Lethbridge). In some parishes the local beverage was so bad that the good-natured parson begs to be excused from characterising it… the Vicar of Plympton St Mary says 'An answer to this might be attended with ill consequences'. Knowstone had 'poor, hungry cider' and nearby North Molton's was 'poor meagre cider'. One wonders whether a individuals' rights to freedom from molestation in their own homes can be said to have given stimulus to American colonists: their fight was not only about taxation but also about freedom. Second, the investigative techniques in diagnosing the cause of Devonshire Colic are known throughout the medical world, and can be seen as leading the way for huge life-saving advances in public health.

Let us look at the picture given by Marshall (*Rural Economy of the West of England*, 1796). He makes a contrast with Herefordshire and Gloucestershire orchards which were found on arable and pasture land; Devon's were mostly around the houses, or planted in the shelter of steep-sided valleys. Trees were probably provided by a landlord to his tenant, either produced by him or a nurseryman. In a few places there are cherries, pears and walnuts, but apples (for cider) predominate; very few 'kernel' fruits' 'In the management of nursery plants, the most remarkable circumstance is that of training them, with stems not more than three or four feet high, a practice which is so different from that of the other fruit-liquor counties…' He gives these trees a name 'Damnonian'. He asks whether this result of use of crab stock was to avoid wind or to get fruit to mature near the ground. He concludes that it had simply become the custom. Distance between trees is a statute rod (5.5 yards), compared with John Worlidge's (1691) 7 yards, and 8-10 yards that would later be adopted for standard trees. Such spacing makes no allowance for intercropping, so perhaps that practice had waned. Do we know about the practices of tree planting? Certainly on wetter ground there emerged the use of ridges or mounds – sometimes still visible and confirmed by archaeological aerial photographs. (Although the practice of way [road muck] spreading might confuse the eye.) Trees were unstaked and protected by faggots of brambles, brushwood or furze which was replaced when it rotted away. Grown cattle, sheep and pigs are prohibited from the orchard at all times; horses might be allowed to run through in the winter and calves in the spring. Prior to the gathering season the sward might be cut with a sithe [sic] – an often neglected task.

The uniqueness of Devon's orchards was demonstrated in the Exe Valley with many small garden orchards and 'Dumnonian' trees, ie small and closely planted. As Marshall

> **DEVONSHIRE COLIC**
>
> Devonshire Colic was first described by a learned Exeter doctor, William Musgrave, (b1655), in his 'Dissertatio de arthritide symtomatica'. Doctor John Huxham of Plymouth, described the symptoms: stomach aches, vomiting, muscular and bone pains, paralysis, and death in rare severe cases. With most occurrences in the Autumn, Huxham noted the coincidence with the drinking of cider, blaming acidity in the fruit and drink.
>
> It was a third doctor, George Baker (born 1722, Modbury), who said the symptoms seemed like lead poisoning, noting that over-acidity might cause diaorrhea, but seldom anything worse. By investigating the records of the Royal Devon and Exeter Hospital (opened 1741) in a model of epidemiology he concluded the problem was lead in cider. Lead was used in the joints and lining of mill troughs and cider presses. Evidence came from a lead-lined press in Alphington, with a paper, published in 1767. Practices changed and the colic soon disappeared.
>
> However, not everybody agreed at once. William Marshall (1796), perhaps with his tongue in his cheek, attributed colic to an illegal spirit distilled in a porage pot and known as 'necessity'.
>
> For those who could afford it, the treatment was six weeks in Bath. The place had two beneficial effects: one wasn't drinking cider, and the hot baths aided the removal of lead from the body's system.
>
> In international medical circles the word Devon conjures up lead poisoning. Ian Maxted wrote a paper on colic appropriately called 'Etched on Devon's Memory'.
>
> Over and over again, the promotion of Devon's cider in the late nineteenth and twentieth century stresses the healthiness of the drink and its beneficial effects. The drink needed defending against something risky about the county's drink and the acidic apples produced in its orchards.

From Cider Tax to Brexit

Legislation has played its part in the fortunes of Devon's orchards.

The Excise Bill, commonly referred to as the Cider Bill, of 1763 was one of Lord Bute's proposed measures to reduce the much-increased National Debt after the Seven Years War. The tax of 4/- per hogshead was on cider at point of production, (rather than point of sale, as in previous liquor taxes), and excise men were to be given general rights of entry and search in private domestic properties as well as commercial ones. It led to a famous quote from William Pitt about cottagers' defiance; the tenement's roof may shake, the wind may blow through it, the storm may rage, the rain may enter, but the King of England cannot enter.

The tax was unpopular. In the cider counties of the West Country and Devon there was not only rage but violence. There was a riot in 1769 when John Russell, fourth Duke of Bedford, visited Exeter. The 'No cider Tax' mob barricaded him in the Cathedral.

Lord Bute resigned (probably the most Devon-orchard-related political resignation), but the tax was introduced in modified form by his successor George Grenville. Later, after the Napoleonic Wars, the duty was raised to 10/- per hogshead. After the War, William Pulling who had moved from Berry Pomeroy to Ledbury in Herefordshire, chaired a meeting of dissent in Totnes in 1816. Orchards were cleared as a result, according to Rydon.

Cider duty was abolished in 1830, and apart from a re-instatement between 1916 and 1926 was not reintroduced until 1976. There was an increase in 1984.

The legislation is the Alcoholic Liquor Duties Act 1979 with associated orders and regulations. The Act defines cider and cider perry as a beverage with 1.2% to 8.5% alcohol obtained from the fermentation of apple or pear juice without any additives other than those approved by Customs and Excise. Significantly for Devon's orchards, those producing up to (originally) 1500 gallons, and now 70 hectolitres (7000 litres) per year are exempted. Unless production and consumption is non-commercial, exemption must be applied for, and Customs and Excise must be advised if sparkling cider is to be produced.

There has been an issue of the strength and cheapness of 'white' ciders, and their attractiveness to alcohol abusers. In the Autumn Budget 2017 the Chancellor announced that there would be a higher rate of duty on ciders between 6.9% and 7.5% alcohol with effect from February 2019. Most white ciders are now produced outside Devon, and local producers of higher alcohol cider have protested that their sales will be hit by an added charge on what is already a relatively high-priced product.

approached Somerset the stems of the trees increased in length, by Wellington becoming full-stemmed *English* orchards (Marshall's italics). So Marshall's picture is not one of a 'traditional Devon orchards' of high 'standard trees' with stock, usually sheep, grazing the sward underneath.

Conclusion

By the end of this period Devon's orchards had grown into a huge phenomenon. This was vastly bigger than the expansion driven by a growing and wealthier population, new tastes in food and drink, money from new overseas trade or a substitute for awful beer. It almost seems to have no reason: an ignorance in growing, a huge surplus, and an ignorance in use – remember I started the chapter with my reference to the tulip mania. But it happened. Around every farm, hamlet, village and town of Devon were vast acreages of orchards, transforming the look and life of the county. The consequences concern the rest of the book.

Mill at Fairlinch, Braunton.
(Tim Potter)

Ch 7
Cider Country

With only occasional references to Devon's orchards up to the fifteenth century, and limited information for the sixteenth and seventeenth century, the Dean Milles's Survey in the middle of the eighteenth century provides a comprehensive, if not complete, picture. Nearly a century later the Tithe Survey fills the gaps, showing Devon to be a cider county. Before that there is suddenly a flood of information. Fraser, Lyson, Marshall, Polwhele and Vancouver, all names familiar to those researching the agricultural 'revolution', have significant things to say about Devon's orchards

Robert Fraser wrote a report for the Board of Agriculture in 1794 (Fraser). He seems more interested in the future role of another apple, the potato, on Devon's farms. But he acknowledges the omnipresence of cider (every farm had an orchard of apples and occasionally cherries, pears and walnuts) and the economic importance of cider, particulary to some southern parishes. While many cider makers were not bothered about apple varieties, choosing apples on the basis of quantity of juice produced, he dismisses the story of adulteration with turnip juice. He notes the improvements in cider making in some places – in the neighbourhood of Exeter, Chudleigh, Newton Ferrers, Paignton and Totness [sic], aided by the use of improved milling machines. Cider has 'a richer flavour of the apple' than in other counties. In Staverton fermentation is stopped by repeated racking off to produce a sweet cider, and he commends the cider from there.

He notes that 'Several gentlemen plant nurseries for apple trees, and give the plants to any of their tenants who will engage to inclose a piece of land for an orchard, This is a system well deserving the notice of all the proprietors in the county' (and is presumably one that has the potential for increasing rents). Given the suggestion that tenants were free to engage in the scheme one wonders what was in it for them. Both parties must have seen the production of fruit and cider as more productive and profitable than the alternative arable or pasture. Vancouver (below) says Lord Clinton provided an orchard rather than an area of pasture for the tenant's cow. One reads into this that orchards were still expanding.

William Marshall's *Rural Economy*, mentioned in the previous chapter, divides the county into parts and describes each in turn (Marshall). To summarise, Devon's orchard practices are so widely distinctive 'as to appear pretty evidently to have had separate origins'. The distinctions are many. First there is the size of the orchards; they are farm and village orchards and therefore small, but second there are so many of them because of the large number of farms, so that the aggregate acreage is considerable. On both points he is certainly supported by the Tithe Survey of c1840. Third he notes situation; some orchards on water meadows and north facing slopes had never paid for themselves, but the steep-sided valleys, not suitable for corn or meadow, make good sheltered situations for orchards, and trees can flourish on stony soils. This point confirms that many orchards in Devon were a relatively new phenomenon and that the planting of them was not embedded in an age-old culture of land use. Fourth he is intrigued by the practice of tree-raising, and the results. He confirms what Fraser has said about landlords supplying tenants, but also notes the existence of nurseries, and that farmers produced trees for their own use (or their neighbours), and that cottagers produced them for sale. This suggests a considerable industry of tree production and real demand for planting new orchards. Fifth, he says 'In the management of nursery plants, the most remarkable circumstance is that of training them, with stems, not more than three or four feet high'. Could this Devon practice be an inheritance from growing fruit trees on hedgebanks now extended into orchards? And what does it say about the common view that 'standard' orchards are traditional, allowing grazing under the trees? However, he is very impressed with the planting achievements (in West Devon), saying orchards are kept in a state of perpetuity. 'As the old go off, young ones are planted, in the interspaces, without any apprehensions of miscarriage'.

Richard Polwhele's *The History of Devonshire* of 1806 includes an account of the rural economy, and notes the importance of cider for a number of parishes, including comments on its production. There is not enough information to obtain a picture of orchard practices.

Charles Vancouver's *General View of the Agriculture of Devon* dates from 1808 (Vancouver). This is a thorough survey, district by district, with a section on improvements at the end. He notes that in the 'free or dunstone lands' (presumably the Culm Measures) Lord Clinton attaches to his tenements a small orchard, sufficient to produce one to two hogsheads of cider, plus 'hoarding' apples; this replaced grazing for a cow; so cider for milk! His account of how orchards are established does not tally with William Marshall's. He says that after cider-making it was the practice of spreading the pulp or cheese with a rake or harrow over a small piece of ground. The most vigorous of the resulting seedlings were allowed to grow on to the sixth year (with the pruning of heads), and then they are planted out on the eastern side of a hill 25ft or 30ft apart in holes previously made. In the hole will have been deposited about two seams or horse-loads of road-scraping or way-soil. Such practices could soon produce orchards that were of bigger trees than the 'low, scrubby, crab stocks' of William Marshall, and the spacing supports this. He advocates planting varieties of trees of the same sort together so that the fruit will ripen together and can then be milled, 'expressed' and fermented together; this is better than mixed fruit fermentation. This seems like a move to 'traditional' orchards as we know them.

The New (1811) Edition of Tristam Risdon's *Chorographical Description or Survey of the County of Devon* acknowledges the importance of orchards, and that for some the return from them pays the farm rent (Risdon). This answers my questions earlier on, suggesting a substantial trade in cider and fruit. However, he says 'The orchards are not either so large and productive, or so numerous as they used to be. The cyder tax operated to reduce the number of apple trees, thousands of which were cut down at the time it was imposed, and the produce of the remainder is probably lessened by a variety of causes, among the principal of which are, the unfitness of old orchard ground to the growth of fresh trees, and the known gradual decay of some of the best varieties of apples'. This is a less bullish account of orchards than Marshall and Vancouver. The orginal Cider Tax of 1763 was defeated, but taxation was slipped through later. The Napoleonic Wars saw taxation on foreign wines to the advantage of native drinks, but these did not escape tax either. Certainly viruses can explain the deterioration of varieties.

Samuel Lysons (in 1822, *Magna Britannia*) notes that great quantities of cider are made, with record exportation in 1820; 11,265 hogsheads (at 64 gallons per hogshead that is over 700,000 gallons) from Exeter, Teignmouth, Dartmouth and Salcombe (Lysons). It was sent to London, Newcastle, Sunderland, Leith, Swansea, Liverpool and thence by canal (Leeds & Liverpool) into Yorkshire. Knowing the canals of northern England quite well it had never occurred to me that they may have once transported cider from Devon. And the drink would have been exported too. There emerged an important set of merchants to organise this huge trade from farm to distant places. Lysons also notes the importance of cherries from the orchards of

Bere Ferrers and Goodleigh.

This is probably a good point to stand back and review our knowledge of Devon's orchards at the end of the Napoleonic Wars before advancing to the information revealed by the surveys instigated by the Tithe Commutation Act of 1836. We can divide our review into things we know and things we don't know.

The literature confirms Devon as Cider County. There was a huge acreage, totalling well over the 22,000 in Herefordshire, confirmed by the later Tithe Map. There were big geographical variations, with the South Hams and the east of the county being most productive. While cider making was carried out 'domestically' on the farm, the surplus meant that many villages and farms in these areas were involved in substantial trade, particularly of cider, locally and by boat to other parts. Merchants had emerged to organise the trade, an example being the Pelling family from Berry Pomeroy who traded from Totnes, and who organised local opposition to cider taxes. This was big money, for example enabling significant harbour improvements at Paignton. But trade was not constant because of variations in crop yields and other factors. There is evidence of landowners encouraging new planting of orchards. The county's orchards reflected the nature of its farms – they were widely scattered, small, and were mixed with other farming activities. Likewise the standard of orchards and cider making varied considerably from farm to farm. There is no evidence of widespread interest in new fruit varieties or improvements in cultivation, and those who are raising the standards of cider making are singled out for mention. Just as indicated by Milles's respondents in 1757 there were plenty of conservative and lazy practices. We have already seen how the Napoleonic Wars at the start of the century had benefited the domestic fruit and drink market. High tariffs had been imposed on imported fruit after the Wars (1819), to continue protection of the domestic market, leading to an expansion of orchard planting of dessert and culinary fruit in Kent in the 1820s and 1830s, and presumably the same applied in Devon.

Lowering of tariffs on imported fruit in 1837 had probably come too soon to have much impact on the orchards recorded in the Tithe Survey. Tariff on apples was reduced from 4s per bushel to a 5% ad valorem duty which was equivalent to between 3d and 7d per bushel. One result was that American apples flooded into the country; 120,000 bushels into London alone in 1838 (Short). This led to orchards being grubbed up in Kent, 'displanted' was the euphemism, and a Parliamentary Enquiry (Harvey).

As for things we don't know, were orchards at their most abundant? Risdon talks of orchards being cleared, but how widespread was this, and why is it not picked up by other commentators? The post-War return to French wines

TITHE COMMUTATION ACT

The Tithe Commutation Act of 1836 can be seen as one of the last stages in the disappearance of a medieval tradition. Payments to the Church in kind were replaced by monetary payments – a calculation with information on land ownership and use for Devon, and for the rest of the country. This provides a standardised overview of agriculture, field by field, at one point in time. The arbitrariness and incompleteness of surveys like those of Dean Milles are replaced with standardised and complete information.

John Bradbeer has described the two elements of the Tithe Survey. The first is the Tithe Map, 'a large scale plan of the parish with each parcel of land marked and numbered'. The second is the Tithe Apportionment, 'a listing of all parcels, their land-owner, present occupier, field name, current land-use and area (in acres, rods and perches). The usual ordering in the Apportionment is alphabetically by landowner. The land-use required to be recorded were arable, meadow, pasture, gardens, orchards, woodland, buildings and waste' (Bradbeer).

There are just two points on the land-use of orchards that need to be made, First, there is the issue of when does a garden become an orchard? Second, when does an orchard cease to be one?

reduced sales at the top end of the market, while reductions in labour force would have reduced demand at the other end. Devon's cider merchants found it difficult to shift all their production, and some read significance into the move of William Pelling to Hereford. Improvements in cider making equipment, particularly mills, meant that less fruit was required. It all points to a reduction in need for orchards.

Tithe Map Information

The Tithe Commutation Act is described separately. Thanks to the Devon History Society (DHS) analysis we have a table giving orchard acreages in each of Devon's 470 parishes, with a percentage of each parish's total area. The total county acreage is given, distinguishing between 'old orchards' where there is a discrepancy between the name orchard and current non-orchard land use, and 'orchards' where there is no doubt that the main land use is fruit growing. There are 3842 ha (9494 acres) of old orchards, and 43,457ha (107,382 acres) of orchards. It needs noting that these are only the tithable orchards; many garden orchards would be excluded from the survey, so the county's total orchard area would be more than the 15618.43 hectares (38,594 acres). That amounts to 2.55% of the land uses recorded. Even with exclusions this is a huge total, suggesting there were more orchards in Devon than was realised from other estimates like Samuel Lewis's, or did the Tithe Survey perhaps inflate the total by including decayed or former orchards? DHS analysts tried to overcome this by excluding land with an orchard name but with alternative use.

It is hard to take in this huge sum – very crudely that acreage of modern orchards could produce 2 to 3,000,000 tons of apples (– at today's prices of over £100 per ton the crop is worth £0.3 billion). Admittedly a few parishes grew mazzards, and some had dessert fruit, and of course yields were tiny by today's standards, but nevertheless the total is huge. What tonnage would there have been in a bearing year, and how much cider could be made?

In the table below I have highlighted the ten parishes with the highest number of orchards. Although the original Tithe measure was acres, DHS Summary findings are in hectares. I have converted these back to acres.

		Hectares	Acres	
1	Bere Ferrers	216.81	536	9.09%
2	Broadclyst	202.15	500	5.27%
3	Paignton	175.84	435	8.52%
4	Ottery St Mary	165.81	410	4.29%
5	Cullompton	156.07	386	5.23%
6	Halberton	149.07	368	4.92%
7	Dunsford	148.15	366	6.12%
8	Colyton	144.54	357	5.09%
9	Sandford	137.48	340	4.35%
10	Uffculme	132.02	326	6.11%

How do these compare with Milles guesstimates of eighty years earlier? Only one, Paignton, appears in Milles's 'top ten', but others might if there had been responses. There were only Milles's Survey responses from five, with no replies from Broadclyst, Cullompton, Halberton, Dunsford or Uffculme. Milles says that Bere Ferrers has 'many orchards and cherry grounds' (the big cherry trees took up a lot of space) producing 2000 hogsheads. Paignton was thought to have over 300 acres by Milles, making 4000 hogsheads (– the Tithe records an increase to 435 acres). Ottery, where the Tithe figure is 410 acres, Milles has 'some hundreds increasing every year'. The Milles respondent in Colyton gives no acreage but estimates cider production at 1500 hogsheads per year; this suggests a significantly smaller acreage than there was eighty years later. Likewise, Sandford had about 150 acres which had grown to 340 (137.48 hectares) by the time of the Tithe Survey. There is thus real evidence that in many places, and for the county as a whole, the acreage of orchards had increased between Milles and the Tithe.

I have looked at how 'top fifteen' parishes from the

Milles's respondents were placed at the time of the Tithe Survey. The Tithe Survey shows increases in orchard land in ten cases and decreases in five. Many Milles's responses were crude guesstimates, but the evidence points to an overall increase in orchard acreage over the eighty years. The one significant change is Tavistock which shows a huge fall from a 200 acre estimate in Milles to 45 acres in the Tithe. John Wynne's mid-eighteenth century plans of the town show an abundance of orchards. Copper was found at Mary Tavy in 1796 causing a building boom in the town, with the Bedford Estate leading the way in new developments, and it is clear that orchards were sacrificed. For example, the villas (c1820) along the new Plymouth road sit on the sites of former orchards, but perhaps this loss was made up with new orchards in nearby parishes.

What does this tell us about the distribution of orchards? Taking these 'top ten' parishes plus a further nine with over 60 hectares we come up with the following picture (in order by area).

Bere Ferrers. The parish is on a peninsula between the Tamar and the Tavy. The area was known for growing cherries as well as apples, explaining the large acreage. It was easy to distribute the crop by water to Tavistock, Plymouth and the very active mining enterprises in the area.

Broadclyst, along with Woodbury, Whimple, Ottery and Sidbury (all with 100+ hectares) forms an arc of orchard growing parishes to the east and southeast of Exeter.

Paignton is the only 100+ hectares parish in the South Hams, and this may come as a surprise given the frequent mention of the area's orchards up to this point in time.

Cullompton (over 100 hectares) with Uffculme shows that orchards were common in the Culm Valley, and we can add to them Halberton and Thorverton stretching west to the Exe Valley.

Dunsford and Tedburn St Mary constitute a separate area to the west of Exeter, and they can be linked to orchards in the Creedy Valley, Sandford and Newton St Cyres, just to the north.

In the east there are large numbers of orchards in Axminster, Colyton and Chardstock parishes.

John Bradbeer has looked at a sample of 53 parishes across what are now the districts of Torridge and North Devon. He found 1612 acres of orchards, or 1.2% of agricultural land, compared with 2.55% for the whole county. (The acreage would have been higher if non-tithed garden ground had been included.) They were widely distributed, although a few of the more exposed parishes had tiny acreages there were none without any, (Challacombe had just 0.01%). He has a diagram which suggests that there was a higher proportion of orchards on the Carboniferous Culm Measures (to the south and west of Barnstaple) than on the Devonian rocks to the north. It would be easy to attribute this to the apple's dislike of cold, wet soils and poor drainage, but arable crops don't like these either. It could be that the higher arable acreages of the better drained areas meant there were more cider-drinking agricultural workers (and therefore more orchards) than on the stock-rearing areas further north. And of course the proximity of the Barnstaple market would be an additional factor. 85% of orchards were less than an acre in extent, and only 0.7% of orchards were of more than 3 acres; an average-sized orchard was 0.58 acres. Mazzard greens were larger: 1.59 acres. 'The orchards were usually situated close to the farmstead and comprised part of a complex of small parcels, rarely more than 1.5 acres in area, which surrounded the farmstead. These other small plots typically have names like 'Calves Plot' or merely 'Plot' and were used for pasture and it is likely that orchards too were similiarly used by livestock' (Bradbeer).

Ahead of the DHS Orchards Project K. C. Turner had looked at the Tithe Assessments for Alfington, just north of Ottery St Mary. He writes 'The Tithe Assessment Records were an accurate account of orchards in 1850. Before this date the situation can only be guessed at by the few records available. What we do know is that the Alfington Tithing, consisting of Holcombe Barton and Rock and Mayne Districts, had a total of 861 acres of recorded land, of which 72 acres were designated as orchard. Included in these 43

THE DEVON ORCHARDS BOOK

> **ORCHARDS ACREAGES ON THE CULM**
> **DEAN MILLES'S SURVEY and TITHE SURVEY**
> **COMPARED**
>
> Dean Milles sent out his long questionnaire to incumbents in 1757. There was a response of 57%, but not all questions were answered. There was a question on orchard acreages. The Tithe Survey (1837 to 1841) was more thorough and specific, and the answers are more exact. The acreages given here combine orchards and gardens, so this is not an exact comparison with Milles.
>
> John Bradbeer's spellings of parish names are used. Parishes in brackets are omitted in the total.
>
> | | DMS | TS |
> | --- | --- | --- |
> | Abbotsham | 20 | 28.35 |
> | (Alwington | Small quantity | 41.91) |
> | Ashford | 30 | 14.54 |
> | Brendon | 1* | 11.06 |
> | Charles | 10 | 33.37 |
> | Heanton Punchardon | 60 | 74.75 |
> | Huish | 10 | 14.23 |
> | Huntshaw | 20 | 31.40 |
> | Landkey | 150 | 221.07 |
> | (Loxhore | Not many | 22.62) |
> | Luffincott | 10 | 13.77 |
> | (Mariansleigh | Nescio | 50.09) |
> | Meshaw | 23 | 27.35 |
> | Pancrasweek | 15 | 30.22 |
> | Tawstock | 200 | 263.45 |
> | Trentishoe | 4 | 12.13 |
> | Welcombe | 15 | 14.12 |
> | TOTAL | 568 | 789.81 |
>
> *Incumbent adds 'which I desire you'll come and measure'.

parcels of land, were 22 acres listed as arable or pasture, but referred to in the Tithe record as Apple Bin, Hill's Orchard, Old Orchard, Great Orchard, Baker's Orchard and Goveton's Orchard. This indicates that by now almost a third part of the orchard land had undergone a change of use and as each acre of orchard contained an average of 100 trees, two thousand two hundred trees had already been taken out. The decline was underway' (K. C. Turner). All analysts of the Tithe Assessments will be familiar with this situation of parcels of land with an orchard name not actually being used as an orchard. Of course orchards are not like permanent ancient woodlands – they were planted, sometimes grubbed up and sometimes replaced with new orchards elsewhere, but Turner is perceptively right in noticing more loss than replacement.

Devon's Distinctiveness

The Tithe Survey tells us about size of the orchards and their precise location on the tithe map. Frustratingly, at the time of writing, the intention of mapping all the orchards electronically was awaiting South West Heritage Trust's big task of drawing all Tithe plots. So one can't compare a mapped form of orchards in each parish as one can with Ordnance Survey maps at the end of the century. Instead one can use the work that has been done in individual parishes like Braunton, Dolton and East Budleigh and the work of John Bradbeer. What comes across is the number of very small orchards in different ownerships; many are what we would call garden orchards today. So most settlements were not only surrounded by them, they were penetrated by them to the very hearts of the settlements. They surrounded most farms. Away from farms there were free-standing orchards too, but significant work would be required to see if some of the advice on planting location (such as steep combes or eastern sides of hills) was followed. The Tithe also tells us about their worth in comparison with other land uses, (– their use cannot change, other uses can).

What do we know about fruits grown? By far most of the trees were apples, with cider the destination. From contemporary descriptions of Devon cider it is clear that distinct cider varieties had emerged – fruit that would stay long on the tree with high tannin. Culinary and dessert apples and apples for 'hoarding' were grown near the larger town markets. Mazzard or cherry gardens occupied significant areas east of Barnstaple and beside the Tamar.

What do we know about apple varieties that were grown and new introductions? The Tithe Survey doesn't help with this. There are a few varieties that we know about, such as Tom Putt, but Tanner is dismissive in saying that varieties, particularly cider ones, cannot be enumerated because of the local names. Dessert, culinary apples and other fruits would find a corner in the farm orchard. The bigger houses such as Killerton were growing fruits already brought in from other parts of the country. John Garland, gardener at Killerton writing a generation later lists Cox's Orange Pippin, King of the Pippins, Blenheim Pippin, Cox's Pomona, Lord Suffield, Frogmore Prolofic, Lady Henniker, Peasgood's Nonsuch, Stone's Apple or Loddington, Warner's King, Winter Hawthorden, Bramley's Seedling, Dumelow Seedling.

Room For Improvement

The Tithe Map doesn't tell us about the state of the national cider trade which was becoming dire by the middle of the century. Henry Tanner's *Farming of Devonshire* 1848 is extremely critical of the cider orchard growers and cider makers syndrome. He says that the growers don't differentiate between varieties, supply mixed loads of fruit to the cider makers, who then can't make good ciders, or aren't prepared to. So there was a lot of bad cider, and the market turned against it. Tanner is very dismissive about Devon's apple naming, and one wonders what has happened to the named varieties of the previous century. This points to a disincentified activity. Tanner does have time for nurseries, but their concern was not with cider apples; they were more interested in the tables of the big houses and the greater discernment in dessert and culinary fruits amongst the growing middle classes. The movement to produce wine-matching (or wine-beating) ciders with particular cider apples had slipped away, and by the middle of the nineteenth century cider sales were in serious decline.

As a postscript it is worth noting the Paignton Harbour Act of 1838. There was need for a harbour to export cattle, cider and 'the famous Paignton cabbage'. It was built, with a cider store nearby, so that orchards have indirectly contributed to the county's infrastructure. And also of note is that the Hunt family were named as instigators; their descendants still make and sell cider today.

Conclusion

Samuel Lewis's *Topographical Dictionary of England* states that at the start of the nineteenth century there were 23,000 acres of orchards in Devon, just a thousand more than Herefordshire, and probably an underestimate. On the precedent of the Milles survey we are safe to assume that most were cider orchards. The population of Devon in 1801 was 343,001. Around a century later in 1894 there were slightly more orchards, 26,000 acres of cider orchards, but the population was on its way to doubling – 631,808 in the 1891 Census. By the time of the Tithe Survey had too many orchards been planted?

Age of Press at Fairlinch, Braunton. (Tim Potter)

Now recreation, once cider makers' supply line: Staverton railway.
(Peter Rodd)

Ch 8
Seeds of Decline

In 1866 the Board of Trade (later the Board of Agriculture and then Ministry of Agriculture), started a survey of livestock and crops, soon including orchard acreages, known as June 6th Returns. As with the Tithe Survey the orchard statistics have to be treated with caution. The Tithe Survey probably erred upwards by including decayed orchards, while the June Returns only applied to registered holdings and orchards of an acre or more, thereby reducing the total significantly for Devon with its small orchards. By 1877 the total was c9300 hectares, (23,000 acres) just ahead of Hereford with 22,000 acres. So we have the total of 15,600 hectares of the Tithe Survey followed by an apparently huge decline, and this compared with a national increase in orchards from c57,000h (141,000 acres) in 1873 to 96,000h (236,000 acres) in 1904. Devon was never to match the total of the Tithe Survey again; it can be seen as the zenith of orchards in the county.

The Devon and Exeter Horticultural Society was inaugurated early, on 19 February 1829, and there was an ongoing debate as to whether its function was to raise the standards of the glasshouses of the big estates or the gardens and orchards of the humble cottager. At one of the early meetings of the Society Sir Thomas Acland proposed the holding of an October show 'considering the importance of the apple in Devonshire'. Others pointed out that 'the state of our orchards is anything but creditable', and hoped the exertions of the Society might lead to a better order of things. Leading nurserymen were very involved in the Society, so presumably it benefited them (Caldwell). Nationally, in 1851, there was clarification of fruit nomenclature thanks to Robert Hogg (*British Pomology, The Apple*), leading in 1854 to the Pomological Society with Hogg as Secretary and Joseph Paxton as President. There were orchard and fruit trials, a Fruit Committee, huge exhibitions and awards. Advice on what to plant commercially followed in the *Fruit Manual* (1860) and enthusiasm for the development of new varieties. But inevitably there resulted a specialisation in a limited number of varieties that were considered commercial, as noted by John Garland, gardener at Killerton, writing in the 1880s: 'Thirty years ago, many of the finest sorts of apples were entirely unknown in the orchards of this part of the West of England, but they are now grown by hundreds of thousands, and are in great demand.' He attributes this to good prices in city and town markets, and knowledge disseminated by local November shows which had become widespread. Talking about varieties he likes 'free bearers', not small trees like Hawthornden or Tom Putt without sufficient bearing surface. He talks of 'handsome apples' by which he seems to mean quite large, but includes Cox's Orange Pippin which is of 'medium' size. Some apples like Cornish Gilliflower are lovely but profitless, and therefore best for the private table. Good prices are obtained for early apples: Lord Suffield, Frogmore Prolific, Loddington and Warner's King, but the best prices are for those stored to March when all sorts are scarce: Bramley's Seedling and Dumelow's Seedling. This would have required careful storage in cool, dry, dark rooms.

So with efforts at improvement how do we explain the orchard decline? On seeking the causes we will look at the conservative state of Devon's mixed farming and challenges to long-term development of orchards, at social changes and the decline of traditional outlets, at the neglect of new markets for fruit and cider, and finally we will look at the short term advantages of orchard disposal. However, the decline must be kept in perspective; there were new developments, particularly of fruit growing beside the Tamar and Tavy and the start of factory cider making. Devon remained a massively orcharded county.

Conservative Farming and Challenges to Long-Term Investment

Henry Tanner wrote his 'Farming of Devonshire' in 1848. He comments that 'Valuable as the orchard is to the Devonshire farmer (and its worth may be very much increased), it is remarkable that so little attention is bestowed upon it either in the selection of good varieties or in the manufacture of the cider'. He sees big variations in the productivity of different orchards and the performance of different fruit varieties, and the real problem is 'the indiscriminate mixture of apples is a very negative part of the manufacture of cider'. He criticises this 'indiscriminate' mixture not only because it doesn't take account of varietal variations but because apples that are not 'ripe and mellow' are mixed with those that are. It was such a lost opportunity; 'we should reasonably anticipate as much variation in the produce of the seasons and localities in this country as we find in the vineyards on the continent'. But how 'reasonable' (to use Tanner's word) was it to expect mixed farmers to become 'craft' cider makers? We've never expected wheat growers to know all about flour milling, and were the vintners of the continent also growing arable crops, managing a dairy herd and fattening lambs?

There has been a debate about the contribution of the system of 'life' tenancies (and tenancies of three lives, or 99 years were common) to the lack of improvement in Devon's farming in the nineteenth century. Incoming tenants borrowed to pay the substantial upfront payment or 'fine', so they had little money for improvement, while the landowner with money in his pocket had little interest in making improvements either. This led to a farming system that was 'ignorant, undercapitalised and old-fashioned'. Robin Stanes challenged the universality of this view. Gradually leases for a term of years replaced life leases, and all were accompanied by management covenants which would include orchards (Stanes). 'Preserve and manure apple trees' and 'Apple trees replaced and manure' are examples from the Bluett and Bedford Estates. So we must look for other reasons.

Another disincentive to investment was the mid-century decline or depression in agriculture. The repeal of the defensive Corn Laws in 1846 led to a gradual decline in arable farms and a conversion to stock rearing and dairying, with an associated diminution in the agricultural labour force, cider consumption and the need for orchards. Arable farming had the practice of paying workers with cider, and of being particularly generous with cider at harvest time: less workers, smaller families, less cider, fewer orchards.

Another way of looking at this is price. In 1878 *White's Directory* records that over the previous twenty years the value of the cider had decreased by 50%. As for table fruit, the bulk of the English crop was passed over in favour of bushels of cheap, attractive French, Canadian and 'Yankie' apples. Imports from across the Atlantic quadrupled between 1875 and 1879. Electioneering in his Hawarden constituency, Prime Minister Gladstone urged farmers to plant fruit instead of corn to reduce the five million that had been spent on fruit and vegetables in 1879 alone. Then at the turn of the century there was the refrigerated import of fruit from Australia, New Zealand and South Africa (Morgan). Domestically, transport favoured concentrated production and economies of scale.

The other important point to stress is that Devon's small farm orchards were not a good basis for industrialised cider making. Rachel Evans talks of 'regrators' or fruit buyers who took possession of cherry orchards on the Tamar for a season for a fixed sum. Likewise merchants would buy farm-produced cider and sell it on. There are quite a few listed in *Kelly's Directories*: twenty one in 1883, twenty five in 1893, nearly all in the South Hams (– perhaps the Directory concentrated on them). A few of the merchants

SEEDS OF DECLINE

pursuits' its main thrust has been perceived as improvements to stock, and mechanisation. Orchards and orchard products have been more prominent with the Bath & West. Devon was also slower into agricultural education than many counties, and conservatism persisted.

Social Changes and Decline of Traditional Outlets

Cider had replaced unpalatable rye beer in many parts of Devon, so it did not have to achieve very high standards to be regarded as an improvement. And then there was adulteration ('thinning and doctoring' was the Herefordshire expression), which applied to cider sold in London and other places. There were common stories of turnips being added to the apples, and beet added to strengthen the colour. It had been common practice to add water. It was Hereford, not Devon, that tackled this issue head-on, with Henry and Percy Bulmer's pioneering factory processes leading to a resurgence in cider making. The

Cows, possibly at Warlands, Totnes, c1900. (C. F. Rea. Bruce Church Collection, Kingsbridge Cookworthy Museum)

are also listed as manufacturers. The very term 'manufacturer' is interesting – just two in 1883 and seven in 1893. The trend was for fruit to be taken from the farms to a factory. One senses that farmers were growing fruit and making cider at a proverbial great distance from their market. Scattered small orchards with irregular cropping were not what the merchants wanted. Certainly this was not the age when the producer jealously guarded his 'premium product' and indeed it was the merchant as middleman who was the main beneficiary in relation to input.

The Devon County Agricultural Association was set up and ran the first County Show in 1872. This was well behind the Bath & West. Although the Association's objects were the 'advancement of agriculture and encouragement of education and knowledge of agriculture and country

Cider apples awaiting milling stored on orchard floor, Warlands, Totnes 1901. (C. F. Rea. Bruce Church Collection, Kingsbridge Cookworthy Museum

63

TREE PRODUCTION

Orchards cannot exist without the production of trees. Prior to planting out the trees will have been raised in a nursery. There are different practices and contemporary accounts (Chapter 7) cover these. Many trees destined for cider orchards were little more than selected seedlings with unknown varietal characteristics and were therefore un-named.

However, if they are named varieties they will probably have been produced by a specialist grower who has taken scion material from the different parents, grafted them onto rootstocks and 'nursed' the infant tree.

Having observed this practice amongst contemporaries I am amazed at how it must have been conducted by farmers and gardeners centuries ago. Without special knives, wax, tape, bamboo canes, labels, waterproof markers, printed descriptions and illustrated catalogues how did they do it? Furthermore the nature of the business required trading skills of quite a high order. Visiting Normandy in 1993 we met a professional 'greffeur' who cycled on his butcher's bike, grafting trees to order. Was he following a very ancient tradition that pre-dated nurseries? For me this is one of the biggest mysteries and achievements of this story.

Four practices of tree production developed in Devon. First, cider makers could divert their pomace from pig food, spread it in the orchard, and use the resulting seedlings ('gribbles') as their supply of new trees. Second, this could be done on a larger scale and the resulting trees advertised and sold; the local press was full of advertisements, and this seems to have been common. Third, there were specialist tree nurseries which would stock fruit trees, including named varieties of apple and rarer fruit, destined for the gardens of the larger houses. This trade crossed boundaries. Fourth, there was the opportunist identification of seedlings, like the Royal Wilding.

Lucombe and Pince's Exeter Nursery produced Lucombe's Pine around 1800, and Lucombe's Seedling was also sold as Kirton Fair in 1831. Veitch's Nursery produced their Perfection around 1865. Later Stevens of Sidmouth produced Woolbrook Pippin, Woolbrook Russet and Lloyd George. Cider maker R. J. Hill of Barkington Manor, Staverton, introduced Brown's Apple and Paignton Marigold between the Wars.

Totnes cider trade diminished. A less acknowledged aspect of the cider trade was the use of the drink for adulterating imported wine. With the easier import of bottled, labelled wine there was less opportunity for this cider outlet. Sabine Baring-Gould told the story of how a Devon merchant was asked for his excellent cider to be told it was all now retailed by a London merchant. The London merchant told the prospective purchaser that he didn't sell cider, only champagne (Baring-Gould). This amusing anecdote says three things: first, there was some good cider; second, that it wouldn't command a sufficient price so was sold as champagne; and, third, that the producers were completely at the mercy of the sellers.

Paying wages in cash rather than kind (cider) under the Truck Act of 1887 meant that many rural employers had less incentive to own orchards. Exactly how firmly this Act was enforced was a matter of debate, but it was seen as significant. Marshall's verdict on many farm workers as 'drunken, idle fellows' shows that the impact of cider drinking was a heated subject, but there were such expectations amongst the workers that farmers maintained the tradition. The growth of the temperance movement is known to have had an impact on alcohol consumption in the second half of the nineteenth century. There is no doubt that teetotalism was popular with Bible Christians while open-minded Primitive Methodists preached abstinence. Bands of Hope were widely established after 1874, and Meeting Rooms of the Order of Rechabites were common.

The stories of Methodists who didn't touch alcohol, 'except for cider', are so common as to ring true. While the temperance movement might only account for the disappearance of some orchards, it undoubtedly contributed to decline. Whiteways, with their non-alcoholic 'cydrax' were to address the issue.

Neglect of New Markets

We know there was a big rise in national population in the nineteenth century – huge in the industrialising areas with a relative drop in rural areas. While Devon's population was rising overall, it was the towns and the coastal resorts that explain this growth. Many left the farm and villages for the towns, or emigrated. Agricultural workers were less in demand because of recession in the farm economy and the start of mechanisation. Also there was a decrease in family size, from eight to four children over the century. In the villages there was a reduction in tradespeople as many manual craft activities were replaced by mechanised processes in the towns. The farm and village orchards made the cider that fed the farm and village workers, and less was needed. In the towns, and in other parts of the country, beer was often drunk more than cider.

Cider had benefited from the trade disruption of the Napoleonic Wars – it became a replacement for French wines either as product or medium of adulteration. The post-War sustenance of Corn Laws meant that high barley prices for a while impacted detrimentally on competitive beer. Corn Law abolition meant there was barley prices were steady for decades, and between 1857 and 1900 national beer production doubled from 18million to 37million barrels. Cider production had remained static and relatively left behind.

Cecil Torr in his *Small Talk at Wreyland* talks about how agriculturalists in Devon failed to see the impact and potential of the arrival of the railways (Torr), and the county had to wait for Whiteways of Whimple in the twentieth century before the cider industry matched Hereford in rail use. The Bere peninsula took advantage of railways – but the railway's lateness (1890) meant it was virtually the twentieth century before the benefits were felt.

It would be wrong not to record the impact of great houses on fashions of table fruit. Orchards became a more aesthetic part of the large-house garden (often part-decorative) and new varieties would find their way into domestic gardens. Large houses were wanting originality for dessert, rather than any form of standardisation which the

KILLERTON AND POLTIMORE ESTATES

John Garland, gardener, Killerton, wrote hints from practical experience with the encouragement of Thomas Dyke Acland. He notes a big increase in growing of fine apples not known thirty years ago, and local November shows have spread the knowledge. He recommends varieties (not favouring local ones), with great stress on the market: high prices for early apples and storage for late high prices. He talks about markets in great cities, opened up by rail. The availability of sieves and baskets and need to pack in straw to avoid bruising is important.

The description of the Poltimore Estate in 1907 provides an interesting picture of orchards on a great estate at the zenith of country house culture. Two criteria governed their management – appearance and productivity. The grounds looked good, and this included kitchen gardens and glasshouses, so that family and guests would be impressed. And that good things were going on extended to entries in shows and exhibitions, locally like the Devon and Exeter Horticultural Exhibition and nationally like the Autumn Shows of the Royal Horticultural Society.

While apples for the table was priority, there was an astonishing amount of produce. Some of this may have been sold commercially, exemplified by Lord Poltimore winning a prize for 'one bushel of a culinary apple and half a bushel of a culinary apple packed ready for market' in Exeter in 1893 – competing with professional nurserymen.

commercial growers wanted. However, estate owners and gardeners were competitive, and prizes at various shows were coveted. At the 1893 Devon and Exeter Horticultural Exhibition Lord Poltimore won second prize for 'one bushel of a culinary apple and half a bushel of a dessert apple packed and ready for market'. This class received more entries from commercial growers than the big estates and suggests that estates were happy to enter the market.

Short-Term Attractions of Orchard Disposal

As villages and towns expanded there was a need for land. Orchards on the edge of expanding towns were most vulnerable as they would command good prices. We have already shown that the Bedford's town expansion destroyed many orchards in Tavistock. Paignton lost many in a less planned way. The name 'orchard' on long-established buildings and streets is the give-away.

An underlying factor was farm amalgamation. An example is the farm of Vinnicombes at Trusham, having 53 acres in 1851. Over the subsequent decade land was amalgamated with the neighbour, excluding orchard and pound (Cameron). The new owner would not want duplication of cider making arrangements, and all over the county small presses and associated orchards were abandoned.

Where railways arrived in a village they were likely to cut through orchards on the edge. At Braunton it was the centre, where the Barnstaple to Ilfracombe line affected dozens of orchards, dividing them, and separating many from easy access to presses in the village.

New Developments: Tamar and Tavy

The area on both banks of the Tamar, and to some extent the Tavy, had for centuries been a fruit and vegetable growing area for Plymouth and Devonport. Produce was taken to the city by boat three times a week, with many growers (or their wives) accompanying the produce to the pannier markets (Evans). However, new local markets were developing with naval ship building, repairs and victualling at Devonport and Plymouth, and many new mines upstream. It was the arrival of the railways which opened up vast other market potential. Topography tended to favour the Cornish side and the Bere peninsula for growing, but when the railway eventually arrived it was on the Devon side, with stations at Bere Ferrers and Bere Alston, and in

The Barnstaple to Ilfracombe railway (1874) severed orchards at Braunton.

1908 a branch from Bere Alston crossed into Cornwall with stations at Calstock and Gunnislake. There began a remarkable scramble for land, for all sorts of horticultural produce – a very distinct landscape in which orchards found their place. Woodlands on the steep slopes were cleared, and fruit (particularly strawberries), vegetables and flowers, interspersed with apples, plums and cherries, all commanded a premium price nationwide for earlier crops than Kent and the east of England – but essentially a twentieth century story.

New Developments: Factory-Made Cider

The hope of matching French wines with cider had not been realised. With declining rural sales, a poor image and social suspicion it needed entrepreneurial skills to bring orchards and cider making in Devon up to date. Beer making at Burton on Trent had shown the opportunities. Pale ales, easy to store and transport, had grown massively at the expense of traditional ales, with a flourishing export trade. Major breweries were developing the concept of tied houses, particularly in the new conurbations. Cider had no equivalent. Some new public houses tied to breweries were grand in architecture with an air of respectability, but the cider houses were the antithesis. Bulmers of Hereford had the vision to drive forward cider making in a new way, and Herefordshire was to seize the advantage of fast growing markets in the West Midlands and South Wales. Perhaps the problem for Devon was that its main cider makers were long-established and scattered. They saw themselves as merchants rather than manufacturers, responding to the market rather than creating one. Henleys of Abbottskerswell, Hunts of Paignton, Symons of Totnes, Teign Cider of Netherton all expanded over the period, but merchants is how they described themselves. For a county with a huge surplus of orchards this meant that a continued decline was inevitable.

Conclusion

So what was all this 'improvement of orchards' that exercised the county so much? If you 'improved' the orchards when cider sales and fruit prices were declining what was the point? Right from the time of the Milles Survey, the need for improving cider quality had been recognised, and the county had always struggled to produce top quality table fruit. And it was not only Devon that had problems. In Kent it was observed that 'the man who sticks a tree in the ground and expects, without proper care and attention to obtain good crops, the man who grows the wrong varieties, gathers the fruit at the wrong time, packs it in the wrong way, and sends it to market at the wrong time, will never make fruit growing pay' (Harvey). But in Devon even more expertise was required – fruit had to be turned into a cider that could compete with a rejuvenated beer trade. One concludes there was a problem of structure, and if the structure of the fruit producing and using activities was all wrong (with small, scattered, unspecialised mixed farms as its base) could you improve, or hadn't you better start all over again?

The story of Whiteway's, to be described in the next chapter, shows how the entrepreneurial skills of one family had enormous impact. But they followed Bulmers and Hereford. It was not the growers or the agricultural improvers that found a new place for orchards in the West, it was manufacturers who saw new forms of manufacturing, new markets, new ways of reaching them, developed new products, new packaging, and new forms of promotion.

We should stop and ask what orchards in Devon looked like. Most would be cider orchards of standard trees, and many would be in poor condition. East of Barnstaple there were mazzard greens. A glance at an Ordnance Survey map shows them everywhere, and totally integrated in farms and villages. Aesthetically these were orchards at their loveliest. Near the towns there would be fruit farms of better managed trees, while garden orchards in the bigger houses had reached a high point of cultivation.

Remnant orchard beside houses, Lobb, Braunton. (Tim Potter)

Ch 9
Near Disappearance

When H. Rider Haggard undertook his tour of rural England in 1901 he painted a sad picture of Devon at a time of agricultural depression. Farmers wanted protection from overseas goods, they had little spare money for improvements, and their cheap and poorly housed labour was quitting the countryside in huge numbers. As for orchards they were 'very ill-cared for… to the eye which has first studied those of Kent'. He visited a farm of 400 acres between Honiton and Exeter containing 25 acres of cider apple orchards; in 1900 the owner had sent 15 tons of apples to market for 17s6d a ton, out of which he had to pay for gathering and other expenses. The orchards would go, with a few retained for domestic purposes. A nearby farmer said of cider in the 1920s that 'I paid 'em to make it, and I paid 'em to drink it, and still the beggars aren't happy. So I stopped making it' (K. C. Turner). So no sales, and no satisfaction from making your own cider: why keep your orchards?

Much of the decline noticed in the last chapter continued. Looking at the century there will be five main themes. First, the consequences of improved global and national transport meant that Devon's orchards were subject to further competition from elsewhere. Second were continued changes to farm economies; the move to more 'efficient' mechanised farming with specialisation and abandonment of a mixed farm economy with orchards. Third there was the effect of two World Wars. Fourth there was the accelerating trend towards factory-made cider (made elsewhere) with fruit supplies from large modern orchards. Fifth, there was emerging a differentiation between the 'old fashioned' standard orchards of the farmhouse orchards and the very different orchards planted to the specifications of cider makers and fruit farms. Specialised and professional fruit growing at last started replacing the mixed farm orchard.

The Government's 'June Returns' of crop acreages give a general indication of the way things were going. From 8949h in 1925 there was a modest decline to 8555h in 1945 with a huge drop to 3949h in 1965 (of which only 2215h were commercial) and the tiny 385h in 1985. This was the nadir and the often quoted figure used to claim that Devon has lost more than 90% of its orchards since the War. There has been a modest rise since then (468h in 1995), which has continued since. Perhaps the most significant Return is that for 1965 when 1734h were grown commercially, and 2215 were not. Jumping ahead to 2005 there were 806h in the county – on 721 holdings, making the average just over one hectare, and this is after the exclusion of the smallest orchards from the Return: enough said!

Competition from Elsewhere

We have dealt with this issue in earlier chapters, and it was, of course, a national rather than specifically Devon phenomenon. Fruit growing continued as part of many mixed farms rather than as a specialisation, and mixed farmers only took an interest in fruit when grain, livestock and dairy prices fell. Fruit, in any case, had never promised reliable profits – there was a surplus of cider apples, and table fruit's seasonal advantage was losing out to continental fruit in the summer and southern hemisphere fruit was in the spring.

Abandoned fruit farm (Devon Rosery and Fruit Farm Ltd), Cockington. (Tim Potter)

Completely overgrown fruit farm Bramleys, Cockington. (Tim Potter)

The demise of North Devon mazzards fits in with this story. This tiny cherry, delicious in prime condition, but having huge labour requirements and a short season, could never stand up economically against many tropical fruits, whether fresh, canned or frozen. The same is true of the more versatile Tamar cherries; there is just one Devon orchard left at Lamerhooe, and the fruit is not harvested. All sorts of apples, dessert, culinary and cider would still have been found in most farm orchards in the early years of the century. Fruit farms, growing a range of dessert and tree fruits, were attempted across the county, and their remains can make an interesting piece of 'orchard archaeology'. At Halberton during the First War an enterprising fruit merchant from Bury in Lancashire brought a team of girls to harvest local apples, and loved the place (or an inhabitant) so much that he returned to stay and planted a linear orchard of Bramleys on land spare from the narrowing of the broad gauge line. Remains of mazzard trees in a woodland garden above the Taw Valley led to the discovery of apple trees, pears and soft fruit bushes; the living remains of a fruit farm. At Whitestone, beside the Dart near Cornworthy, there are ancient Bramley trees. And at Cockington near Torquay it was a surprise to find a collection of long-abandoned Bramleys covered with brambles. The story of Four Elms Fruit Farm at Newton Poppleford is not a fruit farm in the traditional sense; it is a huge dessert apple orchard where the owners' admirable specialised attention to one fruit, the apple, and the market, shows what Devon can achieve on a good site. The case study of Dartington tells a very different story.

The improved transport that brought apples from other continents also meant that seasonality disappeared. There was no longer the particular advantage (or premium price) of getting early fruit to market. Cherries and short-keeping early apple varieties, with strawberries, from the Tamar lost significance.

Of course, new circumstances provide new opportunities. Improved transport meant that the trend

Last cherry orchard on Devon bank of River Tamar near Lamerhooe, Sydenham Damerel.

towards large units of cider production, noted in our last chapter, continued. The story of Whiteway's of Whimple is covered separately, but there is no doubt that transport made Whiteway's. It was on the South Western Railway's main line. Henry Whiteway inherited his wife's farm nearby and was able to take advantage of rail transport to collect apples from farms over a wide area. Farmers complained of railway prices, but it saved them many hours of carting. And then the railway was used to shift the cider all over the country. Advertisements for the company show the 'Devon cyder express' speeding 'Whiteway's Cyder' to the consumer. But as time went on it was fruit from a diminishing number of suppliers. Introducing his price list for 1910 Henry Whiteway was able, in three hundred words, to introduce the concept of 'apple wine', with purity, medical endorsement, 'exceptional conditions of climate and soil', hygienic methods of manufacture, and royal patronage. But underlying this was the railway, transporting casks and bottled cyder easily to larger markets.

Move Away from Mixed Farming

There was an agricultural depression after the First War, and national production of cider continued to fall. Whiteways had no problem in acquiring apples. 540 farmers were signed up to supply in 1920, and by 1929 the number had grown to 1243. This sounds like good news for the farmers concerned, but one wonders whether they had alternatives? As for the orchards was there enough return to sustain them?

Changes to farm economies, particularly mixed farms,

Cows grazing in standard orchard, Whimple. (Tim Potter)

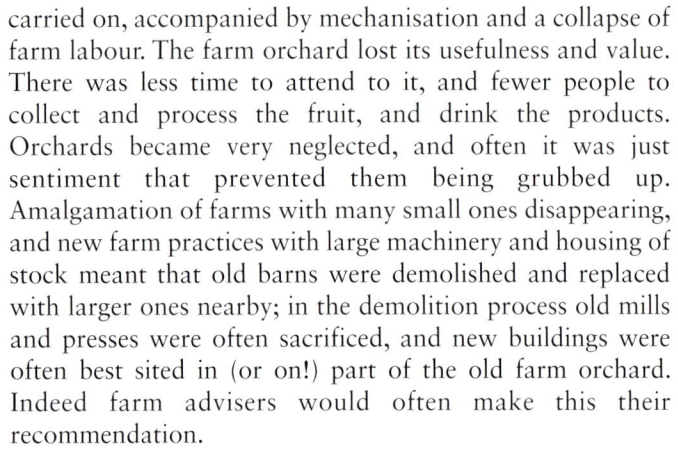

Bush trees, Whimple. (Tim Potter)

carried on, accompanied by mechanisation and a collapse of farm labour. The farm orchard lost its usefulness and value. There was less time to attend to it, and fewer people to collect and process the fruit, and drink the products. Orchards became very neglected, and often it was just sentiment that prevented them being grubbed up. Amalgamation of farms with many small ones disappearing, and new farm practices with large machinery and housing of stock meant that old barns were demolished and replaced with larger ones nearby; in the demolition process old mills and presses were often sacrificed, and new buildings were often best sited in (or on!) part of the old farm orchard. Indeed farm advisers would often make this their recommendation.

There were a number of organisations within Devon, however, that saw orchards as part of 'modern' farming. The encouragement of the Aclands of Killerton in Extension Lectures by both Cambridge and Oxford Universities is an early (nineteenth century) example. The Devon County Agricultural Association established a County Show. Devon County Council had developed a peripatetic model of agricultural education, but this does not seem to have extended to orchard management. Later there were County Technical Centres and a County Council Advisory Service. In partnership with cider makers such as Whiteway's the latter ran courses on management, and Whiteway's offered prizes. After the First War Seale-Hayne was a new Agricultural College, surrounded by orchards and offering courses, but it seems to have been a disappointment to those hoping for an Agricultural Institute advancing all aspects of agriculture across the whole county. Instead it was the growing agricultural advice from the County Council, particularly under John Ross appointed in 1925, with advisory committees that battled for improvement. An Orchards Sub-Committee was set up to revive orchards and cider-making. Later there was a link with Seale Hayne when scholarships were offered for a Diploma course on Agricultural and Rural Economy which embraced orchard management.

At Dartington there was huge investment in orchards,

DARTINGTON

This story is mostly about the last century, but there have been orchards at Dartington, near Totnes, since Tudor times. A lease of 1582 refers to a poundhouse and an orchard called the new Applegarden, probably north of the parson's house. At nearby Weeke part of a meadow was 'now an orchard' in 1606. A lease of 1788 lists several named orchards, and the Tithe Survey (1840) gives a total area of over 65 hectares, nearly 5% of the parish. By 1925 the orchards on the Dartington Hall Estate must have been like many in Devon at the time: 'old, semi-derelict and in a condition that needed attention' said an expert. But to Leonard Elmhirst, looking for an estate to purchase and develop, it was 'a veritable fairy land'; writing to his wife Dorothy he said 'And the gardens and trees you must see for yourself, the orchards, the river and the boathouse'.

Leonard and Dorothy Elmhirst acquired the Dartington Hall Estate to put into effect their progressive views on land use and society, a huge experiment, and the full tale is told elsewhere. Orchards featured significantly in their plans, and what happened to Dartington's orchards over the rest of the twentieth century can be taken as a salutary lesson for those involved with orchards now.

Michael Young, the Elmhirsts' biographer, says that the Elmhirst's experiment was bound to be shaped by the place. Being Devon, orchards featured. There were about ten orchards on the estate, totalling around 30 acres. There were variations in the age and condition of the trees, but they were all old-established standard cider apples, and all needed heavy pruning and conditioning. This was the opinion of Roger Morel, who came with experience from the Dominion Experimental Farm in the Annapolis Valley, Nova Scotia – a big apple producing area, where the activity is called fruit farming. Between 1927 and 1929 'reconditioning' was undertaken, with enough old trees grubbed out to leave space for gapping up with 150 young trees, mostly culinary varieties such as Bramley Seedling and Newton Wonder.

By 1927 there were new plantings as well as 'reconditioning'. Five varieties of plums from Frank Matthews, interplanted with soft fruit, were planted on nearly 4 acres. Next year Pit Park was planted with a variety of dessert apples, (including Cox's Orange, Ellison's, Beauty of Bath and James Grieve), and the following year over 11 acres of young cider apple trees established at Lownard New Orchard. This involved Long Ashton Research Station recommending varieties and the County Horticultural Superintendent advising on planting (including a quarryman to blast holes for the trees). Yarner New Orchard (over 14 acres) followed in late 1932 on similar lines, including one acre of bush trees.

So what was the object of all this activity? The answer must be 'experiment' of the basic trial and error variety. Given how much is known now it is perhaps difficult to appreciate how much ignorance there was nearly a century ago. There were reports on performance: the plums results were 'moderate' (there had been silverleaf), and Pit Park (dessert apples) was a profitable plantation. By 1929 an Orchard Department had been established under Morel. There were then two significant developments made on the basis of experience: a press was acquired and a cider works set up, and a decision was made to acquire land for a larger horticultural unit with commercial and educational objectives.

The Cider-House aimed to produce vintage and high quality cider, but had to buy in some fruit. In 1935 there were experiments with selling apple juice. Sales of cider and juice, 'limited by competition, trade monopolies and the widespread decline in purchasing power', did not match production which was cut back in 1938. The War ensured sales, but a collapse in demand after the War led to the winding up of the operation. As Michael Young said 'Apple juice was no longer in such demand when the juice of oranges and other fruits that had hardly been tasted for six years could again flow down English throats'. Now Dartington Cider Mill means an out-of-Totnes shopping centre, and the orchards are gone.

As for land acquisition there was not universal agreement on the suitability of land chosen at Marley for a fruit farm a few miles to the north of Dartington; 'pasture and light shillet soils at an elevation of 500 feet'. Roger Morel wrote 'The task here is to grow healthy trees that will produce sound fruit, dessert and culinary. A seven year plan for the establishment of these orchards before we can expect profits. Unless in the meantime we can discover a particularly successful catch crop... Fruit trees have many enemies. Fungoid diseases such as canker and scab are prevalent in a high rainfall district...' He was in a sense prophetic. Exposure, rainfall and a workforce unfamiliar with fruit growing all conspired against the venture, and it was without doubt only saved (temporarily) by War demands. In 1951 the whole Orchard Department, both at Marley and Dartington, closed down; most orchards were grubbed up and there are just a few old trees at Dartington that must date from Morel's days.

Orchards are re-appearing at Dartington, but unlike the big projects of the centralised Orchard Department they are small, individual projects in which a productive orchard is sometimes incidental to educational or social objectives, and some are mentioned later.

No orchard enthusiast would look to Dartington in the twentieth century for a model of how to grow or use fruit in Devon, but producing a model presumably was the aspiration of the experimental planting and cider making there before the War. There were lessons to be learned; choose your site carefully, don't rush but grow on the basis of experience, know your product and market, know the technicalities of what you are doing, and above all respect your locale. There is a bigger message: Devon is on the margin of successful fruit growing both in space and time, it can work well, but a fairyland of old orchards is not necessarily a good indicator of what will work well today. The verdict on recent experiments lies in the future.

and while national consultants were brought in there was also work with local advisors. An orchard was planted on the estate with the help of the County Adviser, and then a separate fruit farm on a new site. But the question is begged as to whether this practice was appropriate to small-scale mixed farm Devon farmers. Were these advisors clear in their market for the product? At Whimple Whiteway's were planting new orchards on land they had acquired. Interestingly they retained farms with pigs and a milking herd, so the 'mixed farming' tradition died hard.

By the second half of the twentieth century there were few ADAS advisers who would be interested in advice on improving old orchards. The argument of better land use was supported by grants to grub them up. Jacquie Sarsby says the orchard had been part of the self-sufficiency of the mixed farm, the 'little of everything' which had been the farmer's insurance policy against bad weather, sudden gluts leading to low prices, and the effects of cheap imports. But after 1947, Government 'deficiency payments' or guaranteed prices to the farmer, had become his (or her) new safety net. In the years that followed there were capital grants for such things as buildings, roads and fences, and the farmer was grant-aided to get rid of the 'unproductive' parts of the farm, so that he could become more 'efficient'. As a consequence uneconomic orchards were grubbed out (Sarsby).

The Two Wars

Wars bring together two contradictory approaches: conservatism and innovation. There was a very slight reduction in orchard acreage in the First War, which could be accounted for by recording at a time when 'spare' land was being used for potatoes and vegetables. Despite restrictions on sales, including tax, cider benefitted from a War which saw beer makers facing grain shortages and price rises. But the disappearance of male farm workers accelerated the trend away from farmhouse cider making – to the benefit of factory makers like Whiteway's. Domestic demand sustained orchards in the Second War, but peace brought home the message that decaying farm orchards stood in the way of efficient agriculture.

National Factory-Made Cider Industry

The end of the nineteenth century saw a number of initiatives aimed at improving the state of the cider industry that had in time big consequences for Devon. How much should one read into the fact they were largely outside Devon itself? Herefordshire was the county that responded to new circumstances. Woolhope Naturalists' Field Club organised county a survey, with the outcome a splendid *Pomona*, thanks to the efforts of Robert Hogg as technical editor. The project brought in apple varieties from other places. Then Henry and Percy Bulmer started a resurgence in cider making in Herefordshire by pioneering factory processes which led to improvements in cider production, certainly no more 'thinning and doctoring'. As Hereford trade grew the Totnes cider trade diminished, and Hereford was nearer growing industrial areas of Midlands and South Wales. Broader than cider, the RHS co-operated with the Duke of Bedford with an experimental fruit farm on the Woburn Estate in Bedfordshire. Working with the Bath & West Society Neville Grenville of Glastonbury in Somerset in 1893 started experiments with cider production. This is seen as the forerunner of the National Fruit and Cider Institute which was established at Long Ashton, outside Bristol, in 1913. (The National Association of Cider Makers followed in 1920.)

Whiteway's of Whimple grew up against this background – by its own success and acquisitions it became Devon's only 'national' cider company. Indeed it became more than just a cider maker. But it fits into the story of this book because it stresses the Devon origins of its cider, and it stresses that cider is made from the fruit of orchards. And to emphasise that there must be something superior about cider produced from Devon's orchards it is cyder, not cider. Listen to these claims repeated over and over again in its adverts, but first from a full page advert in the *Daily Mail*, 17 April, 1937. 'Devonshire has the largest acreage of cyder orchards of any county in England.' And 'Whiteway's has the largest acreage of cyder apple orchards in the world.' We seem to be well past any connotations of cider as an unhealthy drink, but just in case they still linger it is interesting to note that cyder is a health-giving product (see Box), and health-giving in ways that would raise modern eye brows

Whimple and Whiteway's are described fully in the Box – didn't Whiteway's have more influence on Devon's

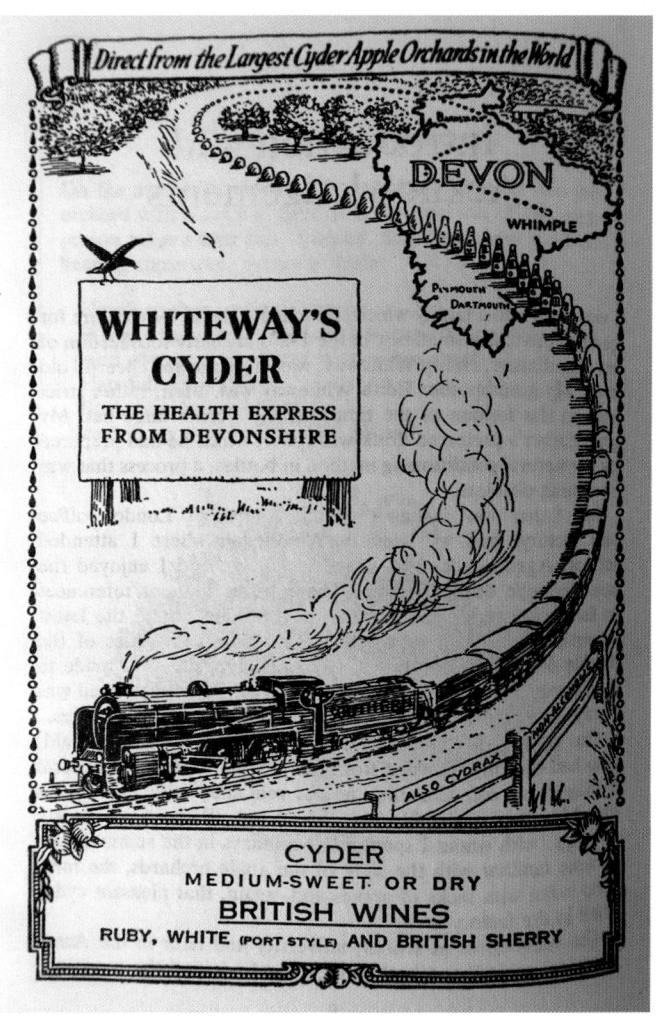

Whiteways cider brings good health from Devon, by train from Whimple.

THE DEVON ORCHARDS BOOK

WHIMPLE

Whimple was the home of Devon's best-known cider, Whiteway's. We look at the impact of Whiteway's on orchards rather than its activities as a firm.

The Tithe Survey shows the parish having 201 orchard plots amounting to 90.92 ha. That's 7.44% of the surveyed land. This puts Whimple into the top league of apple growing parishes of the time; only Broadhempston, Paignton, Plymtree and Upton Pyne had a higher areal proportion. Whimple was part of an arc of much arable land east of Exeter well provided with orchards, where agricultural workers made a big demand for cider, particularly at harvest time.

In 1891 Henry Whiteway came from Harbentonford near Totnes, and brought a press with him. His wife Edith Clift's family came from Churchill, Whimple, and she inherited orchards there. With agriculture in a state of depression Henry moved in 1891 to Churchill with the 'vision of creating a modern and efficient cyder industry together with the scientific orchard management necessary to improve the supply and quality of the orchard fruit.' A tanyard and barn first served as mill and press, and a site by the station provided a new factory with a nearby house 'The Cypresses'. With farm mechanisation and fewer farm workers the Whiteways may have moved at the right time to take advantage of an apple surplus if farms needed less cider for their workers. The family had their own orchards and had no problems in sourcing apples mostly from a 10-mile radius or more, having forty-seven suppliers by 1897, and probably farm-made cider to blend as well.

By 1929 there were 1243 suppliers. Varieties most available were Tom Putt, Woodbine, Crimson King, Kingston Black, Yarlington Mill, Sweet Alford, Sweet Coppin, Sweet Cluster, Star o' Devon and Fair Made of Devon.

Whiteway's desire to improve orchard quality is reflected in annual lists of production and management activity in each orchard. They offered premium prices for particular varieties (such as Woodbine), and offered 'bonus' trees for farmers undertaking new planting. They used their orchards for courses, offered prizes, undertook trials in existing orchards and planted whole new trial orchards. These activities brought them into partnership with different bodies. The 'Ministry' orchard was planted 1935-36 in conjunction with Bristol University's Long Ashton Research Station. Another was planted in 1961 as part of a Ministry (MAFF) cider variety trial; the orchard was called Perry Park, presumably from a previous incarnation. Both orchards contained familiar Southwestern varieties plus newcomers, some from Normandy. In conjunction with Devon County Council's Agricultural Committee there were prizes for growers (based on yields), equipment demonstrations, and courses, such as one on spraying in 1930. Spraying was quite a big activity post-War to the 1960s, some with Ministry supervision.

In 1962-3 the company had acquired another mixed farm of 100 acres at Whimple and planted orchards. By this time the company had merged with Showerings in Somerset who provided the trees. Standard orchards were still the practice, and some of the farm lands were retained for grazing or crops.

In the 1930s Whiteway's started a sequence of acquisitions: Henley & Sons from Abbotskerswell near

Still standing (2017): Whiteway's abandoned Staverton plant.

Newton Abbot, Hele near Cullompton from Schweppes, Hunt's at Paignton, and E. Hill & Sons at Staverton near Totnes. In the pre-War years these orchards, with those at Whimple, produced around 10,000 tons, about 70% of the firm's needs.

In the inter-War agricultural depression farmers welcomed the opportunity to sell fruit to Whiteway's, but not so much with the post-War agricultural boom. Apples were brought from France. There were significant plantings in the 1970s and '80s of Dabinett and Harry Master's Jersey.

After a period of mergers post-War Whiteway's became part of Allied Breweries, and production was moved to Bristol and the Whimple factory closed in 1989. There were still orchard contracts, and most fruit went to Shepton Mallet. When the contracts were terminated fruit found different homes, such as Green Valley Cider, which acquired some equipment and vats before the factory site was cleared.

Whiteway's old orchard at Hele near Bradninch.

orchards than Dartington. In an advert of 1929 Whiteway's claimed to have bought the apples grown by 1243 Devon farmers. And this is before the acquisition of Henley's of Abbotskerwell, Hill's of Staverton, Hunt's of Paignton and Schweppes' at Hele. It is meant as a double endorsement of Whiteway's: the genuine Devon progeny of its apples, and its support of local farmers. However, why should so many farmers have a surplus of apples to sell to a relatively new firm? The answer is, of course, that many farmers were making far less of their own cider than generations before, and therefore had a surplus to sell to Whiteway's. Farm economists often stress the need for farmers to look beyond the production of raw materials like apples to processes like cider making that add value to their produce. It is unlikely that the return farmers were getting from Whiteway's would justify much money on orchard maintenance and replanting, Meanwhile Whiteway's were planting substantial new orchards on land acquired at Whimple. What is somewhat depressing is that Whiteway's, which had been keen to improve standards and production on farms in the 1920s had not raised its own production through to the 1960s.

The Box shows that in the period up to 1960 total production was highest pre-War! Admittedly the Company was then reviewing its orchard quality and considering new planting.

The story of Sam Inch's cider at Winkleigh has huge differences and some similarities. Sam Inch started 'hobby' cidermaking (he was a village postman), in 1917. He produced a good product and he supplied a number of pubs. After the Second War the business had become larger, and in 1988 his son sold it. The new owners developed new products (including White Lightning and Stonehouse), increasing sales massively, like Whiteway's looking to a national market. This apparently alarmed competitors. It was bought by Bulmers in 1996 for a huge sum, closed in 1998 and re-emerged as Winkleigh Cider on a more modest scale, proud of its links to Inch's.

Both cases, Whiteway's and Inch's, seems to show an arbitrariness in the way firms get taken over or sold in our globalised economy. Far-off financial considerations become more significant than local performance or product. Orchard owners with contracts were not really affected, but

Albert Palfrey and Frankie Dennis, Hatherleigh. (George Tucker)

some of those without contracts certainly were. In such a way can remote Board Room decisions affect local orchards and local landscapes.

Late Twentieth Century

If we are to look at the state of orchards in the second half of the twentieth century we have to consider four aspects, agricultural policy, research and training, planning policy and changes to the cider industry (part of which came about because of legislation).

Agricultural policy which emerged across Europe after the War was building on maximisation of production. Michael Winter has described 1945 to '80 as the technological revolution and 1980 onwards as social revolution. Farmers after the War were urged to specialise, and there was huge pressure to do so. The availability of subsidies contradicted the received wisdom of mixed farming which had grown out of a subsistence economy. Which keen farmer could not be impressed by the 1945-80 fourfold increase in wheat yield, 250% increase in milk yield and doubling of cattle and sheep per acre? There was an onward reduction in labour (because of mechanisation in the field and milking parlour), and big structural changes (farm consolidation). Orchards for domestic use or small scale cider making had little place in this, and keeping the orchard only made sense if you had an established market, determined by inertia rather than business reasons. The result was benign neglect or destruction. Smaller fruit farms disappeared. Cider making was static. There was little planting.

Apple Tree Close by Frogmore Village Hall. (Peter Rodd)

Old Apple Yard name, Stoke Gabriel. (Peter Rodd)

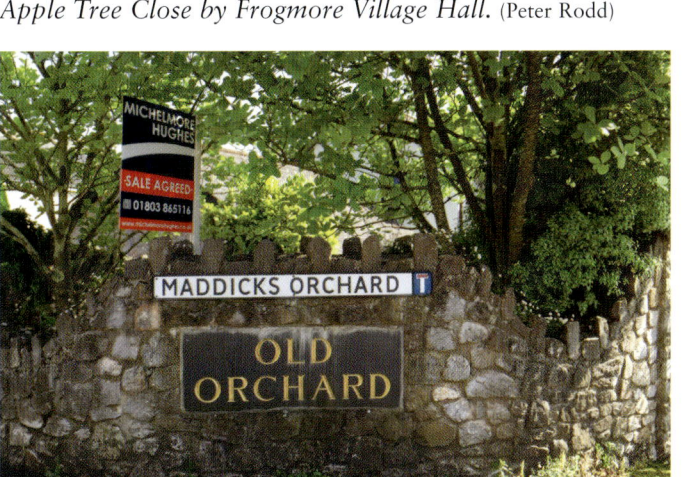

Maddick's Orchard road sign, Stoke Gabriel. (Peter Rodd)

Orchard Gardens, Teignmouth. (Peter Rodd)

Trinnick's Orchard, Ugborough.

Longstem Drive, Dartington. (Tattwa Gyani)

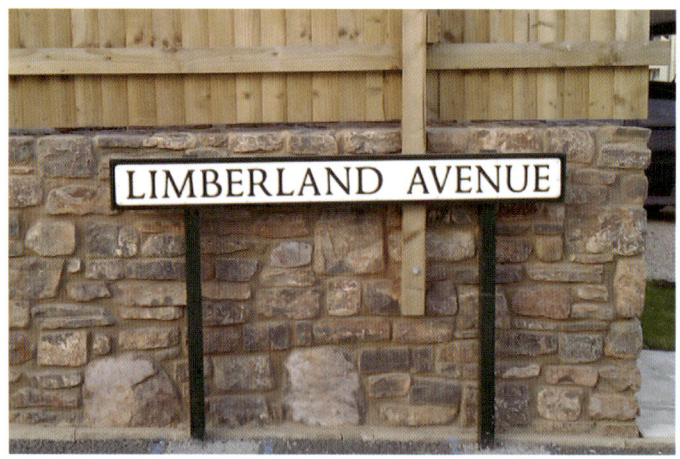

Tremlett Grove, Dartington. (Tattwa Gyani)

Limberland Avenue, Dartington. (Tattwa Gyani)

As for research and training, Devon Farm Institute at Bicton was established by Devon County Council as recently as 1946. It had a Fruit Officer, but its main thrust was to train farmers for the growing sectors. The National Institute of Fruit and Cider at Long Ashton near Bristol, established in 1893, grew out of a private initiative by the Smyth family at Ashton Court. It undertook research and provided advice across the West Country, and its impact was considerable. But for results it needed entrepreneurial land owners and cider makers to respond to its findings and innovations. Other counties were more responsive. It moved away from orchards before it closed in 2003.

New shed in old orchard, Lobb, Braunton.

Planning policy was new. It aimed to curtail Devon's tradition of 'scattered' development by restricting new housing in open countryside unless clear agricultural need could be demonstrated. Land within settlements, such as abandoned orchards, became highly desirable for new housing as the names of new roads demonstrate.

Changes in the cider industry in the latter part of the twentieth century have been mercurial. The imposition of duty in the 1970s had an effect on sales, and the large manufacturers responded by cutting costs (and reducing quality), and one of these was to increase the use of imported concentrates and reduce the links between manufacture and domestic orchards.

Modern Cider Making and Orchards: A By-Passed County

Production of White Lightning started at Winkleigh. It was a cider with a new market, and its appearance would have astounded Sam Inch: a trendy thin plastic bottle contained a high strength (8.4% alcohol) sweet drink. It sold at a low price, and it was remarkably successful, particularly in the Cash&Carry trade. The growth of White Lightning had a huge impact on national cider sales, 8 million gallons in September 1995, making it 7% of national market. In 1995/96 Bulmers bought Inch's for £23 million. Although assurances had been given that production would stay at Winkleigh (it employed a total of 89 people), it was moved to Hereford and most of the equipment at Inch's was moved or destroyed.

While Inch's were supplied from local orchards, White Lightning knew more about imported concentrates. However, Bulmers were interested in using local apples, and advertised for and set up contracts with a number of local growers. Ironically by the time these contracts came to fruition Bulmers only existed in name. The company was acquired by Scottish Courage in 2003 (which in turn became Heineken International). White Lightning disappeared in 2009.

These changes cannot be detached from British membership of the EU and the Common Agricultural Policy. Crudely what was 'common' was a surplus of apple production in relation to demand; in 1995 it was estimated that European production was c10million tonnes of apples against a demand for 7-8million, so as part of the policy of abolishing 'surpluses' there were grants for grubbing up across the continent. Of course fruit trees that have outlived their best productivity require grubbing up anyway, but the policy could be seen as a handshake to those wishing to leave the industry. A decade later the system of subsidy had moved away from production to Single Farm Payments – initially at a rate of £200/hectare for Devon's farmers. In advance it was thought that orchards would be seen as horticultural land use and excluded from the scheme (an issue complicated by Devon's dual use), and there was some grubbing up before rules were clarified and orchards qualified for payment.

At the start of this chapter we suggested five themes underlying the 'Near Disappearence'. It should not be implied that the process is inevitable. Orchards will not return to Devon as they once were, but they by no means need disappear for good. This optimistic note will underlie the rest of the book.

Pollination tree decoration, Killerton Apple Day 2014.

Ch 10
Devon's Orchard Heritage

We began this book by saying how fruit made Devon a paradise, part of Devon's very identity. Our story so far has shown how this was achieved, and how much has changed. Before proceeding to the current revival of orchards and the future, let us appraise Devon's orchard heritage.

Orchard Lore

Probably the best-known orchard tradition is wassailing. This custom, held around Twelfth Night (usually seventeenth January, unchanged from the Julian Calendar), is pretty consistent nationally, although what once applied to all fruit trees is now associated with apples. 'In the South Hams of Devonshire, on the eve of the Epiphany, the farmer, attended by his workmen, with a large pitcher of cyder, goes to the orchard, and there, encircling one of the best bearing trees, they drink the following toast there several times: Here's to thee, old apple-tree, Whence thou may'st bud, And whence thou may'st blow! And whence thou may'st bear apples enow! Hat's full! – Cap's full, And my pockets full too! Huzza! This done, they return to the house, the doors of which they are sure to find bolted by the females, who, be the weather what it may, are inexorable to all interests to open them till someone has guessed at what is on the spit, and is the reward of him who first names it… Some are so superstitious as to believe that, if they neglect this custom, the trees will bear no apples that year' (Minchinton). After a procession with singing a jug or bowl of cider (plus, sometimes, roasted apples) is poured over the roots of a single or higher number of selected trees. This is usually

Whimple Wassail 2014. (Tim Potter)

accompanied by the song. A little boy is then hoisted into the tree to place toast for the birds. Then the evil spirits of the orchard are dismissed with a hullabaloo of gunfire, drummimg, whistling and bashing of ear-splitting implements like tea trays and kettles. Shotgun pellets would dislodge evil spirits in the branches. These elements of tree, song, libation, noise and offerings to birds fit into a wider Western European cult (Minchinton).

There's confusion about St Frankin and Frankin's Nights, possibly 19, 20 or 21 May, including in my North Devon village. Frankin (the spelling varies) was no saint, but allegedly a brewer who vowed his soul to the devil in return for three nights of May frost, thereby reducing the crop and

THE DEVON ORCHARDS BOOK

Cockington Court continues Paignton's large apple pie tradition. (Marissa Wakefield, Cockington Court)

Enjoying the pie at Cockington. (Marissa Wakefield, Cockington Court)

cider yield and enhancing his ale production. Could this be related to the competition between beer and cider three hundred years ago?

If late blossom accompanies fruit on the same bough be ready for death in the family. Do not taste an apple until after St Swithin's Day. And if the apples aren't red enough you need to urinate under the tree.

Marldon's Apple Pie Fair or Festival takes place on the last Saturday in July. The season's first apples are baked in a pie, and perhaps the originator in 1888, George Hill of Marldon near Brixham, was on to a good advertising ploy. He took apples, in a pannier on a donkey, for sale at St Marychurch market. But for the annual fair he organised the baking of a huge apple pie, the size of a kitchen table (so baked in sections), which was paraded in a cart hauled by two decorated black donkeys, accompanied by the village brass band. It was devoured by the villagers with clotted cream. The ceremony died out but was revived in 1958 and continues today.

Sabine Baring-Gould wrote a piece for the *Morning Leader* Amongst the Orchards' and posed the question as to when orchards looked their best, concluding time of fruit rather than blossom. He says 'It is remarkable that, although our peasantry have so many harvest songs they have so few ditties about the apple gathering'. He asked an old journeyman tanner whether he knew any, and just one was produced which it later emerged had been made up in a fortnight by the tanner (and where does this leave others collected by Baring-Gould?).

Winter fruit for keeping should be picked when the moon is waning. When storing fruit the fairest fruit should be picked last – for sale.

The kissing bough preceded Christmas trees – a bough decorated with red apples and mistletoe from the orchard, with a candle. People would pop out on Christmas morning to see the sun shining through the orchards – the sign of a good crop. The Christmas ashen faggot was associated with cider-drinking rather than orchards, with more cider drunk as each faggot was burned through. Finally, in front of the fire could be hung apples on strings that would become roasted before falling into a large bowl of ale beneath, producing the delicacy known as sheep's wool.

In a talk I have given on 'Mazzards' I have asked whether anybody knows the expression 'He's got a nose like a mazzard picker', meaning a hooked nose for hanging from a tree leaving both hands free for picking! Nobody has, indicating a disappearance of common knowledge of cherry picking practices and, indeed, most orchard lore.

Orchard Wildlife

Only recently has there been widespread recognition of orchards' value for wildlife. Orchard trees are usually grafted and then planted so are not a 'natural' habitat. Orchards are not one habitat but a variety – a few ancient and fallen trees in an unmanaged field, huge cherry trees above a lightly grazed sward, young semi-standard trees above machine mowed grass, and so on. Of course, because commercial growers want to both maximise production and quality they resort to disease and pest control – but management intensity varies too.

Snowdrops at Cupper's Piece, Beaford, 1983.
(Photograph by James Ravilious c. Beaford Arts, digitally scanned from a Beaford Archive negative)

Rare for Devon: Golden Eye lichen. (Maxine Putnam)

Many 'modern' apple orchards are made up of high density small trees with short lives (and grubbed up after fifteen years). There are herbicide strips beneath the trees, with mown grass in between. There has been 'chemical warfare' from March to July, but this is giving way to Integrated Pest Management (IPM) which 'seeks to optimise pest control to minimise pest damage and hazards to people, animals, plants and environment'. Even with IPM there is a need for considerable spraying (Marsden). For many cider orchards apple appearance is of less concern so there is less spraying. Other orchards, with ancient trees, shelter belts or relatively high hedges, substantial deadwood, limited spraying because of the long blossoming season, relatively little disturbance, and modest grazing or mowing of the sward are more akin to the habitat of lowland wood pasture. They can be havens for wildlife in the midst of other farm land uses that are less attractive.

Fruit trees in commercial orchards themselves cannot be covered by Tree Preservation Orders. Orchards, per se, cannot be made Sites of Scientific Interest (but they might be

THE DEVON ORCHARDS BOOK

Wild daffodils, Mill Farm, Iddesleigh Bridge.

Below: *Orchids beside a cob nut circle (right), Oak Farm, Wembworthy.* (Jamie Inglis)

for some feature within them). Standard Orchards have been listed as a UK Biodiversity Action Plan habitat.

So Devon's orchards come in different forms, and it would be dangerous and misleading to generalise about wildlife in them. Aware of a shortage of data Natural England undertook a Biodiversity Study of Six Traditional Orchards in England in 2006/2007. Three of these were in Devon. Slew Orchard near Sydenham Damerel, Tavistock, is a south-facing standard cherry orchard on the flanks of the River Tamar. It is thought to have been carved out of ancient woodland in the nineteenth century. Luscombe Farm Orchards and Colston Farm Orchards are both near Buckfastleigh in the Dart Valley, with Luscombe high up in its combe and Colston near the river, areas where orchards were well established in the late seventeenth century (NERR025).

Five key conclusions were made from the study. First, orchards are hotspots for diversity, with a mosaic of

Orchard restoration for horseshoe bats by Devon WildlifeTrust, Hatches Farm, Gunnislake.

Appeal for volunteers to assist in orchard planting, January 2017.

habitats. Second, different orchards have different biodiversity value. Third, with tree removal and replacement orchards had dynamic habitats. Fourth, orchards are part of a habitat 'network' (with hedgerow trees, wood pasture and ancient woodland) that provides continuity of habitat – important for some species. Fifth, some really old orchards (and old trees) were valuable because of continuity. The report says that there were not enough cases to show Devonian characteristics in comparison with other parts of UK.

Apart from the trees themselves, the associated habitats were divided into deadwood, grassland, fresh water and hedges. This division is reflected in an excellent Habitat Management Plan undertaken for the Dartmouth Community Orchard in 2015, suggesting best orchard management practice.

Devon's parkland-like orchard habitats, with lightly managed swards attracting small mammals and insects and those that feed on them, make Devon the northern European stronghold of the Greater Horseshoe Bat, which finds orchards provide good perches for swooping on its favourite foods such as cockchafers and dung beetles. The Devon Greater Horseshoe Bat Project, run by Devon Wildlife Trust, has been assisting the restoration of orchards in the vicinity of bat roosts, and the sight of these bats swooping to catch their food makes the orchards of the county very special. Old and dead trees are good feeding grounds for woodpeckers. Such trees offer nesting opportunities for many birds, including owls, and orchards are important for Little Owls whose decline in Devon may be related to orchard loss.

Guests visiting me from China are excited by lichens, unknown to them because of pollution. Lichens need good light, humidity and circulation of unpolluted air. In December 2007 the spectacular Golden Eye lichen was discovered in a Herefordshire orchard. Since then it has been appearing along the south coast and spreading, liking the twiggy tops of apple trees.

Orchards in the Landscape

Raymond Williams claims that a working country is hardly ever a landscape. He says that 'landscape' is observed self-consciously, with the observer making a divide between the practical and the aesthetic. What is interesting that Devon's non-natural orchards, often quite tiny, should become such a loved landscape feature, sometimes perceived as 'wild orchards'.

Take the Edwardian topographical writer, Lady Rosalind Northcote, and one starts to see the importance of orchards in a different way. She writes 'The (Creedy) valley is a narrow one. And on the hill-sides are copses and orchards, lovely as a sea of pink and white blossoms, and very admirable on a bright day in September, when the bright crimson cider apples, and golden ones with rosy cheeks, are showing among the leaves, and the hot sunshine, following a touch of frost, brings out the clean, crisp, sweet scent of ripe apples till it floats across roads and hedges.' By contrast 'Leading inland from Ilfracombe are lovely combes with their green copses, and ridges of rock, and golden furze, fruit-laden orchards, and slopes of emerald pasture, pitched as steep as house-roofs, where the red long-horns are feeding, with their tales above their heads.'

The original summary definitions of Natural England's six National Character Areas in Devon made no mention of

Sheep, lambs and blossom, Yalberton, Paignton.

orchards. The descriptions of these areas are so broad brush that there is no place for the small-scale, and one wonders whether this doesn't undermine the methodology. The more recent work of Dr Sam Turner on Historic Landscapes identifies orchards as a feature in post-medieval times. The point is made that most are immediately around farms and settlements, and only occasionally do they become a significant element in the wider landscape (S. Turner).

Most traditional orchards were of standard trees in close proximity to the settlement or farm providing a visual buffer between building and farmland. In villages they often provided an outlook from houses. And they were a tangible part of the landscape; you could walk or play in some of them, and you could eat the fruit too; they were and are loved. This landscape popularity is unmeasured, so we are left with 'impressions' from random demonstrations of affection such as opposition to building developments that involve orchard destruction, huge attendances at Apple Days and support for community orchards. We can make an intelligent guess why or what sort of orchards people have in mind when they say they like them.

Today many farm buildings are indistinguishable from industrial workshops. In size, shape, position and materials they seem more alien in the landscape than the traditional buildings they replaced. Many new stock sheds are located on the site of former orchards. New houses on the edge of villages are often built at high densities. There is a strong case for orchard 'buffers' in farm and village, yet I am unaware of orchards planted for landscape reasons. Proposals for green spaces around Exeter may be the nearest thing to it. It is unrealistic to expect orchards to return in the forms of the past.

Orchards for Recreation/Community Use

In terms of heritage it is hard to get a measure of the use of orchards for recreation. There are a few orchards, Lustleigh being the best known, that have been used officially by the public for recreation for some time. The growth of Community Orchards can be seen as a contemporary phenomenon, and so this will be looked at in the next chapter.

There are many orchards that have been used 'unofficially'. Scrumping is the word, and ownership of fruit is the issue. At harvest time many young people of Devon have regarded orchard fruit as communal property, and the stories are legion. Of course matters could get serious with imprisonment; just as an example, at the Ottery Petty sessions on 24 August 1895 William Henry Piper and William Cooper of Sidmouth were both imprisoned for a month for stealing apples. A much more recent case in November 1939 concerned a case at Sidford where word was spread that the proprietor of the Rising Sun, Mr W. G. Morrish, was amenable to people taking fruit from his orchard. This was not the case, the police were called, the orchard was said to be 'swarming with people', a ton of fruit was taken and three adults and four children were charged and fined. This was only a lifetime ago, yet inconceivable now (Barnard).

Vernacular Buildings

Orchards and their products have left behind a range of structures; walls around orchards, poundhouses and related buildings for storing fruit and making cider, cellars for storing cider. A brief account is needed because they are part of Devon's architectural history that would not be there

Drinks manufacturer expands into an orchard, near Buckfastleigh. (Peter Rodd)

without the orchards that stimulated them.

Early orchards were walled, and the costs of the walls at Shute have been noted elsewhere. I am not aware of orchard protection walls that are extant, but there are many old garden walls used for fruit growing.

Once apples were collected most were taken to the pound for making into cider, see below, and some pounds were like a northern bank barn enabling apples to drop into the mill. Large houses, bartons and larger farms needed a dry, cool, mouse-free room to keep fruit for domestic use or market in the Spring. John Garland, gardener at Killerton, made the point of varieties to be stored to take advantage of high spring prices. But where are they? It is surprising how few can be traced. Just as malting floors have been overlooked, so the later conversion of stores to other uses has meant they have not been recognised. There is one at Colleton Manor near Chulmleigh serving a big house, and that at Sutton Barton probably supplied Cullompton market only 2 miles away. As for small farmers or cottagers, the space between ceilings of bedroom and thatch, known as the cock-loft or cock-lart, and entered by means of trap-hatches, was used for storage of 'woordin' awples' (hoarding apples) as well as tatties and onions (Laycock). The establishment of large, mechanised presses on some farms led to a need for more storage; sometimes fruit was taken from bags and spread on the ground, or kept in a basic open silo.

The building(s) where the cider was made was called the Pound or Pound House (– fruit was first pounded or milled and then pressed). It has to be made relatively soon after the apple crop is gathered. So there's the contrast in building requirements between beer made in small quantities all the year round, and cider made in large quantities all in one short season. Beer could be made inside the home. Cider needed a building with a headroom to take the screw press which squeezed the crushed apple for fermentation. Until the nineteenth century the first pressing (or milling) was done in a large circular stone (usually granite) trough around which a horse pushed a stone crushing wheel connected to a central vertical pinion; sometimes these

Ian Batchelor and apple store at Sutton Barton, Cullompton.

massive troughs survive complete or in parts lying around the farmstead. In larger operations they were superseded in Devon in the nineteenth century by mechanical crushers consisting of contra rotating cogged cylinders driven from horse engines. The crushers were usually sited in a loft (also used as an apple store) over the press so that the crushed apple could be fed down to it. In smaller operations a hand-turned 'ingenio' or mill would suffice. The pound house is not a distinctive building externally and is usually only identifiable by surviving machinery. Sometimes it is a building adapted from a different original function, very often a small threshing barn. There is a free-standing early seventeenth-century example at Week, Tawstock, but most are later in date (Beecham).

The visual manifestation of the scale and significance of orchards and cider making is shown in the huge eighteenth-century cider presses still to be found on farms, or (where there is room) museums. Some bear dates, such as 1758 at Fairlinch, Braunton. They can be the height of three men. James Crowden describes one at Burrow Hill in Somerset, but his poetry could apply to Devon. 'Here lies the old press,

The Hunt family have made cider at Paignton since the eighteenth century.

Early nineteenth century cidermill at Yelland Farm, Fremington, with intact fittings. (Tim Potter)

Grade II-listed cidermill at Yelland Farm, Fremington. (Tim Potter)

so vast that some hardly recognise it for what it is or was. A couple of tall screw threads and a bed six feet by six feet, with a small runnel for the juice. These presses are like elephants and just as valuable. Their size, their solidity, their presence lurks in the barn dark. They speak volumes, they are from the age when cider was king and were as highly prized as "Men of War". Greater size means greater pressure, means bigger cheeses, means more juice per cheese, means more cider per man per day'. Apple wood was often used for the screw – from significant trees. It is a pity there seems to be no record of these ancient presses, because once their usefulness has gone their vast size means their preservation is in most cases unlikely. Presses with straw cheeses gradually became replaced by hydraulic rack and cloth presses. Devon came into her own, for a major national manufacturer of these until the 1970s was H. Beare & Sons, agricultural engineers of Newton Abbot; many are still in use.

The next process of cider production, fermentation, requires a lot of space for large barrels. Cellars is the terminology, and just means store, but so long as high temperatures can be controlled the building need not be below ground level. The changes needed for moving barrels at Harford Barton, Landkey, were substantial. Presumably quite a difference between cellars for domestic store and those used by people trading cider.

What is concerning is how much of this physical heritage has gone and is still disappearing. A few pound houses are listed (Yelland), but the mills and presses are disappearing. A few mills have found their ways into museums (for example at Tiverton, Kingsbridge, Sidmouth, Okehampton), and the National Trust houses several (for example, at Buckland Abbey). Occasionally they find their way into other buildings such as restaurants. They are large items, and out of context a curatorial challenge. The original homes of ones that have been conserved are not necessarily recorded. Continued disappearance seems inevitable, but it would to be good to have a record. Many wind and water mills have disappeared, and how valuable a simple record would be. The same applies to cider making equipment – there is a chance to record either from remains or from memory.

Artistic Inspiration

In RAMM, Exeter's Gallery, there is a small oil painting of an orchard by Lucien Pissarro. Lucien, son of better-known father Camille, followed his father's style. He had been brought up by a father who was a respected member of the Impressionist School; he knew Paul Signac and George Seurat and had used Pointillism, making dots or blobs of primary colours to obtain brighter results. Lucien moved to London because of political instability in France and visited Devon on a number of occasions. In 1921 he painted Apple Blossom at Riverbridge Farm, Blackpool, Stoke Fleming. There is a farmstead nestling in the foot of a green combe under an unsure sky, the soil is red, the trees are assuming green verdure, and there is an orchard of fragile, ephemeral blossom. It is an impression, a scene whose light will change very quickly, very Devon.

James Ravilious's images capture the magic of orchards in themselves, both declining standard orchards with their dappled light and twisted shapes, and the more organised recent orchards which are a world of their own. A mazzard tree in blossom at Harford was revisited for its heavenly blossom. James understood that Devon's landscape was a product of man's effort, hard and skilled but often lonely and monotonous work. In his apple harvest scenes he captures the relationship between man striving hard to make a living from trees that do not fruit to demand!

Artist Marcus Vergette works in different art forms, but there is often a link to poetry. He has made cider with poet Andy Brown from Exeter who dedicated his poem 'Devon Apples' to him (see Box). I planned a section on the heritage of apple names, but now I don't need one. Andy takes the Devon apple names and recreates them, while Marcus has made a short film suggesting to me that not just apple varieties but the whole of country life might be threatened.

In *Tarka the Otter* Henry Williamson vividly captures the landscape of North Devon; Tarka and his fellow creatures may be the heroes, but it is the landscape settings that enhance the action. So Tarka swims under the mazzards by Landkey Brook, (right by my garden I reckon), but orchards are not really otter country! For probably the best orchard story, painfully true to one going deaf, is W. N. P. Barbellion's *The Journal of a Disappointed Man*. That village life was not all harmonious is made by Cecil Torr's *Small Talk at Wreyland*; the ingenious theft of apples is beautifully described, and how an apparently trivial act can have profound consequences is the stuff of story telling.

The Reverend Sabine Baring-Gould collected 'a sort of Georgic' telling how the orchard should be managed.

DEVON'S ORCHARD HERITAGE

Apple Blossom, Riversbridge Farm, Blackpool by Lucien Pissarro. (Bridgman Images)

Andy Brown
Devon Apples
(for Marcus Vergette, from 'From a Cliff')

Spring break-up on the frozen river,
the orchard silenced except for the buzz
of insects dreaming this year's apple blossom:
 'Come autumn we'll make cider, next May get drunk...'

*

Longstem's drunk with new ideas,
Blue Sweet knows they trickle down.
Hollow Core turns art in to conception,
Loral Drain has purity of form.

Dufflin celebrates the new millennium,
Hoary Morning struggles with the pasr.
Slack Ma Girdle exploits its possibilities
Keswick Codling isn't much impressed.

Sour Natural is coolly received by the British,
Jacob's Strawberry can't dispel the myth.
Johnny Voun redefines melody & phrasing,
Johnny Andrews' audience laughs & laughs.

*

All Doer says we're in this together,
Ben's Red was raised in the heart of the machine.
Bowden's Seedling never found a job,
Coleman's Seedling thinks the price too high.

Breadfruit have fallen out of the system,
Broomhouse Whites will fret about their debts.
Chisel Jersey trembles on the brink of revolution,
Catshead lays the consciousness to come.

Buttery d'Or witnessed a terrible beauty,
Bickington Grey saw the same thing in Europe.
Gillyflower uttered a cry of defiance,
Captain Broad sent worried letters home.

Honey Pin belongs to a circle of extremists,
Improved Pound plants stories in the patriotic press.
Quarrenden mourns glories past in empires lost,
Goring never insisted on the facts.

Early Bowers were bloodthirsty butchers,
Ellis's Bitter killed for political belief.
King Byerd admired the ancient Romans,
Golden Ball demanded the King's execution.

*

Barum met Beef when each other needed the other,
Beech Bearer keeps a bottle beneath the bed.
Loyal Drong said not to bother looking,
Reynold's Peach found it just below the surface.

Sops in Wine have married and live abroad,
Crimson Victoria had second thoughts about leaving.
Woolbrook feels at home with Sawpit,
Quoinings are ready to be themselves.

Plumverity devotes their all to Cerif,
Stockbear & Sugar Bush find they are strangers.
Queen Caroline always keeps her vigil,
The Rattler rivals her sister's best.

Plum Vite announces the evening menu,
Polly White Hair doesn't bother to dress.
No Pip pays the conjuror,
Morgan Sweet does a graceful turn.

*

Sweet Alford needs the church,
Sweet Cleave plays cards in cafés.
Pig's Nose huffs predictably,
Pig's Snout fits the mouth.

DEVON'S ORCHARD HERITAGE

Sweet Copin enjoys a different perspective.
Tan Harvey comes into her own.
Tale Sweet announces her pregnancy,
Summer Stubbard's Wish was granted.

Thin Skin exerts a mystical pull,
Tom Putt is a person of wisdom & grace.
Nine Square aggravated his heart problem,
Limberlimb was also pale.

Lucombe's Pine let small things slip,
Hangy Down tightened up on them later.
John Toucher was ready for anything,
Long Bit & Listener achieved nothing at all.

Tommy Knight clung to outdated ideas,
Tommy Potter always had the acumen.
Rawlings made final arrangements in silence,
Winter Peach died young – forgive her all.

Billy White lies in the theatre for hours,
Butterbox touches a sensitive nerve.
Oaken Pin kisses your lips,
Sidney Strake takes their final breath.

Top: *Bullocks, Lower Langham, Dolton, 1985.*
(Photograph by James Ravilious c. Beaford Arts, digitally scanned from a Beaford Archive negative)

Above: *Filling sacks, Westpark Farm, Iddesleigh, 1986.*
(Photograph by James Ravilious c. Beaford Arts, digitally scanned from a Beaford Archive negative)

Left: *Cider orchard remnant, Eggesford, 1989.*
(Photograph by James Ravilious c. Beaford Arts, digitally scanned from a Beaford Archive Negative)

THE DEVON ORCHARDS BOOK

Alf Pugsley returns lamb to mother, Lower Langham, Dolton, 1982. (Photograph by James Ravilious c. Beaford Arts, digitally scanned from a Beaford Archive Negative)

W. N. P. Barbellion: *The Journal of a Disappointed Man*

September 19, Early Boughies

Up the village, Mrs Beavan keeps a tiny little shop and runs a very large garden. She showed us all about the garden, and introduced us to her husband, whom we discovered in an apple tree – an old man, aged 76, very hard of hearing and with an impediment in his speech. He at once began to move his mouth, and I caught odd jingles of sound that sounded like nothing at all – at first, but which gradually resolved themselves on close attention to such familiar landmarks as 'Early Boughies', 'Stubbits', 'Ribstone Pippins' into a discourse on Apples.

The following curious conversation took place between me and the deaf gaffer, aged 76, standing in the apple tree –
'These be all appulls from Kent – I got 'em all from Kent.'
'How long have you lived in C-?'
'Bunyard & Sons – that's the firm – they live just outside the town of Maidstone.'
'Do you keep Bees here?'
'One of these yer appulls is called Bunyard after the firm – a fine fruit too'
'Your good wife must be of great assistance to you in your work.'
'Little stalks maybe, but a large juicy appull for all that.'
Just then I heard Mrs B- saying to E- 'Aw yes, he's very active for 76. A little deaf, but he manages the garden all 'eesulf, I bolster 'un up with meat and drink – little and often as they say for children....Now there's a bootifull tree, my dear, that's almost beared itself to death, as you might say.'
She picked an apple off it shouting to poor Tom still aloft – 'Tom, what's the name of this one?'
'You should come a bit earlier, zir' replied T 'Tis late a bit now, doan't ee zee?'
'No – what's its name, I want.' Shouted his spouse.
'Yes, yes, give the lady one to take home, there's plenty for all,' he said.
'What is the NAME? THE NAME OF THIS YER APPULL,' screamed Mrs B., and old Tom moving his bones slowly down from the tree answered quite unmoved –
'Aw the name? Why, tis a common kind of appull – there's a nice tree of them up there.'
'Oh, never mind, 'tis a Gladstone,' said Mrs B., turning to us.
'A very fine Appull.' Droned the old boy.

WREYLAND

One of the old Wreyland houses looked out upon an orchard at the back; but the orchard was not let with the house, and at that time there was no back door. Riding down the lane one day, the owner saw a piece of wood, as long as a fishing-rod, coming slowly out of one of the windows at the back, and going on until it reached an apple on a tree; it caught the apple in a sort of pocket at the end, and then went slowly back into the house again, taking the apple with it. To make quite sure, he waited till he saw this done a second time; and then he went round to the front, and told the father of the family what he thought about his sons, for obviously it was the boys who did it. The father said he would no longer be the tenant of a man who spoke to him like that; so he bought a piece of ground in Lustleigh, and built himself a house.

Small Talk at Wreyland, Cecil Torr.

The Orchard: a Devonshire Georgic

An orchard fair to please,
And pleasure for your mind, sir,
You'd have? – then plant of trees
The goodliest you can find, sir.
In bark they must be clean,
And finely grown in root, sir;
Well trimmed in head, I ween,
And sturdy in the shoot, sir.

The pretty trees you plant,
Attention now will need , sir,
That nothing they may want,
Which to mention I proceed, sir.
You must not grudge a fence
'Gainst cattle, tho't be trouble;
They will repay th' expense,
In measure over double.

To give a man great joy
And see his Orchard thrive, sir.

A skilful hand employ,
To use the pruning knife, sir,
To lop each wayward limb,
That seemeth to offend, sir;
Nor fail at Fall to trim,
Until the tree's life's end , sir.

All in the month of May,
The trees are clothed in bloom. Sir,
As posies bright and gay
Both morning, night and noon, sir,
'Tis pleasant to the sight,
'Tis sweet unto the smell, sir,
And if there be no blight,
The fruit will set and swell, sir.

The summer over-sped
October drawing on, sir,
The apples gold and red
Are glowing in the sun, sir.

As the season doth advance,
Your apples for to gather,
I bid you catch the chance
To pick them in fine weather.

When to a pummy ground
You squeeze out all the juice, sir,
Then fill a cask well bound
And set it by for use, sir,
Oh, bid the cider flow,
In ploughing and in sowing-
The healthiest drink I know.
In reaping and in mowing!

Refrain at end of each verse:
Oh, the jovial days when the apple trees do bear!
We'll drink and be merry, all the gladsome year.

Drink and Food

This chapter is about Devon's Orchard Heritage, and it would be wrong to ignore the heritage of the main orchard product, cider. Devon has had and has a huge number of cider makers, and the list of cider makers in the Box on pages 110-11, (next chapter), will soon be outdated, such is the dynamism of the activity. The list ignores the hundreds or maybe thousands who are making their own drink at home. However, as there is already a substantial literature on this subject there is little point in replicating what is written elsewhere.

So just a few words on what is Devon cider. Devon's heritage may be taste. Liz Copas has suggested that while bittersweets became the Somerset favourite, Devon has more inclined to pure sharps and sweets. The sharps give Devon cider a more acidic flavour – 'dry' rather than sour, with a particularly appley asperity. However, fermentation needs more sugar than many sharps supply, so blending with selected sweets provides the sugar and an addition to the flavour (and aroma) of the finished product. So local cider makers ensured there was a combination of both varieties in the orchards, and some old orchards still reflect this distinctiveness. Of course not all growers would be so discerning, growing 'all-purpose' apples, and some are happy with resulting scrumpy which may be seen as 'heritage' too.

The other point to be made is about the traditional

Left: *Milled apples descend for pressing, Hunts Cider.* Right: *Ready for pressing at Hunts Cider.*

character of Devon's cider comes from its making, but many traditional practices (such as keeving and racking) are no longer pursued. Today most makers will offer several varieties, and a visit to Chris Coles and Nick Pring of Green Valley Cider at Darts Farm, Topsham, will confirm this. They are well placed to pronounce on how a heritage of taste may have translated itself to the modern age.

It might seem odd to mention apple juice under 'heritage'. People must always have drunk apple juice but it never kept for long. Recently juice makers such as George Travis have been developing the idea of varietal juices, so that the heritage of long-established apple varieties is finding a new outlet in the pasteurised juice bottle.

There is a quite extensive, but mostly recent literature on Devon's food, but it has to said that while orchard produce is there, such as apples, plums from Dittisham and mazzards from Landkey, it is hard to find recipes that are particular to the county. The county's Women's Institute has produced recipe books, and a post-War one includes a recipe from Beer for preserving Sweet Alford apples in cider and sugar – the only example of a Devon variety. Devonshire Dumplings have steak replaced by apples in a Sainsburys recipe, so what heritage there? A 'traditional' recipe for Devonshire Apple Cake (apple baked in the cake mixture with none on top and no cider, which feature in Dorset and Somerset recipes), is provided on the web by Bratton Clovelly. A recent WI book has apple flans, sweet omelettes and puddings. Recipes suggest Bramley apples – certainly not a Devon apple, so when did this come about? Interestingly the Bratton Clovelly recipe speculates that sugar replaced honey, but doesn't ask what apple varieties might have been used at the time.

Conclusion: Loss of Heritage

Orchards disappear because nobody wants their fruit. The top challenge for safeguarding orchards must be in finding a return for the crop which justifies the effort of production. In the main this means an economic return, a livelihood, but also in a modest way it can mean other returns such as social ones. Living in a village that has a community orchard the social benefits are obvious. Grants, preservation orders, planting schemes can't sustain an orchard if it has no function, and this will be considered in the last chapter.

Break in Apple picking, Venn, Landkey.
Simon and Becky Houghton and family.
(Tim Potter)

Ch 11
Revival and the Future

There were 860 hectares of top fruit growing on registered holdings in Devon in 2016. (This compares with 1204h in Worcestershire, 1298h in Somerset, 5302h in Herefordshire and 7886h in Kent.) Devon has experienced a growth from 820h in 2010; heading towards double of what was recorded in the 1950s. The figures show 676 registered agricultural holdings growing top fruit, but a significant number of orchards aren't registered. Data should be treated with care. However, the trend is counter to that of nearly two centuries: growth rather than decline. This growth should be set alongside another, that of UK cider sales which have roughly doubled in the last quarter century to £1billion for 2015/16.

Devon's orchards now function in quite different ways, so to understand them better they are grouped as
- a) Orchards serving national or regional cider-makers
- b) Fruit Farms
- c) Orchards serving off-farm cider or juice makers
- d) Orchards used for on-farm cider or juice making
- e) Orchards for home-consumption
- f) Orchards where fruit production is less important.

Orchards Serving National and Regional Cider Makers

In numerical terms (perhaps a score or two of farms) these may only be a tiny fraction of the county's total, but their areas are large. They represent a large proportion of the county's apple production. And they explain most of the recent growth. To understand these orchards we need to talk about the cider makers which they serve, for without them

> **'JUNE RETURNS'**
> The official description says that the June survey of Agriculture and Horticulture is an annual survey which collects detailed information on arable and horticultural cropping activities, land usage, livestock populations and labour force figures'. The data goes back to 1866, just two decades after the Tithe Surveys. There was then a full census every year until 1995 when it decreased to a sample survey, with a full census every ten years. Registered holdings are surveyed. Permanent outdoor crops now only cross the threshold for survey if they amount to more than one hectare. Returns are confidential, and results are not published if individual holdings could be identified.

the orchards would have no raisons d'etre.

First we need an explanation of the link between the grower and the large-scale cider maker. Although it has precedents dating back a century or more there are now contracts whereby the cider maker will specify requirements for orchard planting such as varieties, provide the trees, and sign an undertaking to take the fruit for a number of decades, perhaps thirty years. This was pioneered by Bulmers in Herefordshire around 1968, and then by Taunton Cider in 1975, and they and Showerings (and successors), Thatchers and now Sandford Orchards have all established long-term contracts with growers.

To my mind cider makers are 'national' if they source their fruit from several counties and sell their cider widely too. Over recent decades orchards seem to have lasted longer than many of the larger cider makers, so fast have been the changes. Age and size seems no guarantee of separate existence in the world of the cider making giants.

We have talked elsewhere of the destiny of Devon's own 'national' company, Whiteway's. Let us move on to the geographically nearest 'national' maker of recent decades, Taunton Cider of Norton Fitzwarren near Taunton in Somerset. In the 1980s it was second to the nation's premier producer Bulmers, with over 500 employees producing 30 million gallons per year. Blackthorn was its brand, and it was so successful that for a time this brand overtook Strongbow in national sales. In 1995 it was taken over by drinks group Matthew Clark who later, with Gaymer's Cider, became part of the Irish Group C&C with a big plant at Shepton Mallet (earlier the home of Showerings). In 2016 production and packaging was transferred from Shepton Mallet to Clonmel in Ireland. Although CAMRA claimed that Blackthorn was not 'real' cider on account of its production techniques, including the use of concentrates, Taunton Cider sourced a lot of apples locally. It had agreements with growers on a long-term basis (with a Devon example at Hemyock near Cullompton). Owner C&C has said that it will honour these agreements – production of cider may have moved to Ireland, but fruit will continue to be milled at Shepton Mallet. It is hard to see how a move of production from Norton Fitzwarren to Shepton Mallet and now Clonmel will lead to contracts for new orchards in the future.

The next nearest 'national' name of long-standing was Showerings. This was a family brewing and cider-making

The Corn Barn, Sutton Barton, Cullompton

Yta and Ian Batchelor bought the farm in 2005. They came from Somerset, but Ian's Herefordshire family owned orchards. The farm is just over 100 acres (90 owned, 15 rented). It is rolling terrain with south facing slopes at an altitude of around 70m, and much of the soil is a good sandy loam. It was a mixed farm, including a neglected old standard orchard (1.5 acres).

Yta and Ian developed an organic egg business, but with the market downturn (c2010/11) they were looking for a new opportunity. Family connections made them aware that Thatchers wanted contracts with new growers for early harvesting varieties to extend the cider making season. In 2012 Thatchers offered a twenty-year acreage contract for 6000 trees to cover approximately 25 acres with new varieties Gilly, Jane and Three Counties on M116 rootstock. The performance of these trees will be monitored. They were supplied by John Worle and planted with a post and wire system at a spacing of 9ft x 16ft, (achieving precisely 303 trees per acre). There are also 4000 trees of better-known Dabinett, Harry Master's Jersey, Michelin and Yarlington Mill on M111. The first crop (2015) was 25 tons, then 90 tons (2016) and 160 tons (2017). Acreage has been determined by Yta and Ian's capacity to manage by themselves alongside their mixed farm.

They are pleased to have an acreage contract system which means Thatchers will take a whole crop. The time needed to prune has proved more challenging than expected, and there have been limited problems with disease (canker) and pests. They are no longer 'organic' and are using specific targeted chemicals and traps. They are involved with Stewardship schemes for headlands and traditional grassland in the old orchard.

Sutton Barton has an old apple store and huge ancient barn which, with the orchards, provides a lovely venue for 25-30 weddings per year. Yta and Ian would like to have farm visits, but have found this difficult to organise.

Greeting the bride, The Corn Barn, Sutton Barton, Cullompton.

Orchard Farm

The orchard at Orchard Farm predates the present ownership having been planted in 1977/78 by John Tricks who had a twenty-year contract to supply Taunton Cider. The 42 acre site is south-facing to the east of Cheriton Fitzpaine at an altitude of 160m, with 'every field having a range of soil types'. Taunton Cider supplied and planted approximately 12,000 trees. Most are on M106 rootstocks, with a few on M111. The varieties are Brown's, Coat Jersey, Dabinett, Harry Masters Jersey, Michelin, Nehou, Somerset Redstreak, Taylor's Gold, Tremlett's Bitter and Yarlington Mill.

In 1998, with contract coming to an end, it was sold to Jason and Mark Mills. They negotiated a new contract, soon acquired their own machinery and took advice leading to a more rigorous pruning regime over several years. Production ranges from 400 to 700 tons.

Above left: Harvesting, Orchard Farm, Cheriton Fitzpaine. (Tim Potter) *Above right: Harvesting (close up), Orchard Farm, Cheriton Fitzpaine.* (Tim Potter)

The overall message would be that while national companies provide the security of decent annual payments (lacking in many farming sectors), there can be frustrations with changes of company ownership and a distant personnel that seldom understands farming issues. Premium cider companies and growers often have a really good mutually beneficial relationship based on an understanding of each other's circumstances.

In terms of management, at Orchard Farm there might have been the inheritance of an orchard of twenty years, but this does not mean that management should not always be under review. The orchard has to make sense commercially, but this doesn't mean a slavish following of other commercial practices. Environmentally they have cut down on chemicals (because of expense), have limited cutting of the headlands (and have benefitted from bumblebees), and encourage natural predators. They would like to set up bat boxes, but this is expensive. When visited, following several mild winters, Orchard Farm was suffering from Codling Moth.

There is also a poultry business. Since establishing the farm Jason and Mark have become managers of other orchards at Milverton (in Somerset), Smith Hayne, Stockleigh English and near Crediton. Milverton has carefully pruned trees producing best-ever harvest at fifty-year-old trees, Stockleigh English has been planted with Katy (to produce an early apple for the cider makers) and 'Girls' are being planted for similar reasons near Crediton.

Turkeys, Orchard Farm, Cheriton Fitzpaine. (Tim Potter)
Apples unloading into silo, Orchard Farm, Cheriton Fitzpaine. (Tim Potter)

THE DEVON ORCHARDS BOOK

Harvest time at Wooda Farm.

Apples destined for Hereford from Wooda Farm, Black Torrington, October 2016. (Tim Potter)

Apple crop under contract, Wooda Farm, Black Torrington.

firm of Shepton Mallet which became large following the phenomenally successful launch in 1953 of its perry champagne 'Babycham'. This product can in a sense be seen as instrumental for Devon's orchards losing their nationally known Whiteway's. Showerings success enabled it to take over cider-makers in Somerset (Coates of Nailsea and Magna of Marston Magna) and Norfolk (Gaymers) before the deal which put an end to Whiteway's of Whimple as a separate company.

Another Somerset company with significant Devon contracts is Thatchers. Several generations of Thatchers have been making cider on an expanding scale at Sandford near Weston super Mare, and the firm is still family owned. It owns over 500 acres of orchards, and has around 450 varieties in its Exhibition Orchard. However, a sign of its success, it buys apples from several Devon growers, with recent contracts to farmers at Cheriton Fitzpaine and near Cullompton and Exeter.

Further away, the other 'national' name is Bulmers in Hereford, seen as the national leader from 1887, and it stayed in family ownership until 1970. But it is not always an easy ride in the volatile drinks industry, even if you are the leader. Bulmers was taken over by Scottish and Newcastle who in turn were taken over by Heineken. It has a sizeable product range – Bulmers, Strongbow and Woodpecker are probably most recognised brands. It has about two-thirds of UK sales, and significant exports too. It has a long tradition of involvement in orchards, and this has been maintained through changes of ownership. As well as owning more than 900 ha of its own orchards it has at times had towards 200 long-term contract growers (most in Herefordshire), supported by an advisory service. It has produced its own trees and supplied them to Devon. Bulmers had a big planting phase in the late 1990s, and a more recent second phase ending in 2011. It is proud that 90% of its fruit is locally grown. Devon is a long way from Hereford, but nevertheless in a few locations, such as Wooda Farm at Black Torrington, the Bulmers contract is important.

Of course contracts for traditional standard orchards are ancient history. Today's cider makers' contracts are about low-cost trees on size-controlling rootstocks (M106 or M111). Trees are planted at 300 trees per acre, even towards 400 if topography and field patterns allow it (– pruning of laterals can become more time-consuming if the trees are far apart). The schemes envisage little fertiliser and targeted pest control.

Heavy cropping varieties that are well established in many orchards are Dabinett and Michelin. Under the auspices of the industry there have been efforts to produce new trees with reliability of heavy cropping, good disease resistance and low input requirements, with a wider spread of harvesting dates in October and November. There are 27 varieties of 'Girls', selected after trialling in six counties including Devon. Dabinett and Michelin have been crossed with dessert apples James Grieve and Worcester Permain. Trees with a strong centre leader and an open branching habit to aid production have been selected. (Growers like poplar shaped trees rather than traditional 'goblets', and fruit can be more easily shaken off trees and collected.)

John Worle producing trees in Herefordshire for Devon's commercial orchards.

What about production? One hectare can produce over 80 tons, but 50-60 tons is a more usual figure. Prices paid for better quality cider apples are usually well above £100/ton, say £115, so that produces £7000 per hectare for the farmer with more possible. For the cider maker that means 15,000 litres.

What we have seen over the last few decades is the quiet 'displacement' of traditional orchards by new ones, so that the figures of modest orchard growth in the county in no way means like with like. It is great for farmers as fruit growers, and has needed the large cider makers to promote it. It provides an interesting new appearance to Devon's patchwork landscape.

Fruit Farms

Orchards relating to cider or juice production so dominate the orchard scene in Devon that it is easy to overlook fruit farms. What are they? They are farms that produce fruit, both orchard fruits and soft fruit and sometimes vegetables, for the local market. Fruit might be sold through a wholesaler, but the demise of the local greengrocer and the

WHITESTONE

Riverside Farm is the new name for the farm formerly called Whitestone. The origins of the farm as a unit are quite recent. Apart from part of a barn, there are no ancient buildings on site. Early Ordnance Survey maps show a barn and an adjacent building beside the river, but their small scale, absence of a name and lack of a track to them suggests that the land was farmed from elsewhere.

Edmund, Christopher and David Drew bought Whitestone Farm from George Banbury in 1937. They built a bungalow and planted a fruit farm of Bramleys on semi-standard rootstocks (and standard trees on Holwell). The fruit was boxed with Edmund Drew's name on them.

In 1987 Edmund Drew sold. New owners, the Wilson-Goughs from Harbentonford, extended the orchard significantly and managed it organically, constructing a large cold store The organic apple business was not a success because of crop infestation. In 1992 there was a grant to grub up the young trees under the MAFF Apple Orchard Grubbing Up Scheme, and this work was completed by January 1993.

Cider and juice was made by Tom Burtleson (importing some apples), known as Whitestone 'Old Pig Squeal' with a slogan 'The cider your grandparents warned you about'.

The farm was put on the market and acquired by the present owners in 1994. The apple store was demolished, but the mill, Beare hydraulic press and juice pasteuriser are still in place although Whitestone cider is no longer produced. There are still old Bramleys planted on the Drew's fields, but most of the fields that were planted up by the Wilson-Goughs are now pasture.

The old Bramley trees provided a pleasant background for my niece's wedding, with not a hint of the orchard's turbulent and controversial history!

Wedding Marquee, Whitestone, East Cornworthy.

REVIVAL AND THE FUTURE

growth of supermarkets has challenged this tradition, so there are farm shops, farmers' markets and box schemes.

There are now only a handful of fruit farms left in the county. Our case study shows that it is practicable to run a profitable modern fruit farm in Devon (specialising in one fruit, apples) but competition from other parts of the world is intense.

Left: *Common Ground postcard of modern orchard, East Cornworthy 1992.*

Below: *Compare with postcard: River Dart near East Cornworthy today.*

FOUR ELMS FRUIT FARM

Three generations of the Smedley family have been associated with Four Elms Fruit Farm at Newton Poppleford, adjacent to the main Exeter-Sidmouth road.

A much smaller farm than today's was acquired by Michael Smedley in 1960. There were no buildings, just 25.5 acres in which were grown flowers, vegetables, soft and top fruit. He built a house and developed a Pick-Your-Own business.

In 1993 son Richard Smedley and wife Sue started to supply Tesco with top fruit, and larger quantities were required. Fortunately 32 acres on the other side of the valley became available. A cold store was also required. Since then the PYO site has been sold, the link with Tesco abandoned (too stressful!), prize-winning apple juice has been made, more cold stores (a sixth at the planning stage) and a seasonal fruit shop developed, and apples go to wholesalers and directly to local Waitrose stores – a unique arrangement. The third generation, Mark, has joined the business.

The soils are mostly well-drained sandy loams, of top grade in the west. The valley site is well sheltered, but poplar wind breaks have been planted. The valley-side topography prohibits platform picking, so tree densities are less than on a flat site.

Older trees are planted on rootstock M106 (a few on M104 performed poorly) at 18x10. While still using M106 for about half of replacement trees, smaller trees on M9, M26, P1 and P2 have been planted at 16x6 (100 planted per day with an augur). Trees are supplied by Frank Matthews and John Bridge, who now source trees from Holland and France respectively. The contraction in English fruit farms has had a knock-on effect on nurseries; European mega-nurseries, favouring European varieties, can considerably undercut UK ones. Four Elms had considered using a Devon nursery, but the substantial price difference ruled it out.

Varieties grown are Bramley, Cox, Russet, Braeburn and Gala, with small amounts of Spartan, Worcester and Discovery. Gala is certainly the best-selling variety. Conference and Comice pears have been planted recently for use in a pear and apple juice.

The business has been successful, and a real contribution to the local economy with up to twenty workers joining the family for the picking season. To what can this success be attributed? The farm exudes decades of a very professional approach: planting, staking, disease control, pollination, varietal performance and harvesting have all been scrutinised with great attention to detail, and Richard uses the nice Devon expression to summarise their approach: 'doing it properly'. They have moved with the times, and this has meant constant re-investment.

Regarding the future Richard Smedley is confident that his son Mark will continue to develop the business. On the one hand there was concern that the disappearance of greengrocers was a challenge for their wholesalers, but new opportunities like office fruit schemes had emerged. Their own Devonshire Apple Juice was being retailed by the Co-op. However, the high expectations of the customer, the nature of retailing and international competition meant fruit selling was not easy. With the capital investment now required, he thought it most unlikely that new farms would be established in Devon.

Four Elms Fruit Farm, Newton Poppleford. Blossoming trees on sloping site.

REVIVAL AND THE FUTURE

Looking west at Four Elms Fruit Farm, Newton Poppleford.

THE DEVON ORCHARDS BOOK

Orchards Serving Off-Farm Cider Makers

There are far more Devon cider makers than those listed, and this is because an accommodation for small-scale production; legislation has for some time exempted from duty those cider makers whose production is less than 70 hectolitres (7000 litres) per year. This quantity is held to be too low for profitability as a full-time occupation, and is therefore often referred to as 'farmhouse' exemption, suiting farmers who make cider part-time as well as working a farm. This means that we can distinguish between those who have broken through this ceiling and are operating full-time employment businesses, and those that haven't. The former are likely to purchase fruit from a number of orchards. Companies like Sandford Orchards, Winkleigh Cider Company, Green Valley and Hunt's all purchase from local orchards, and in some cases have orchards of their own.

Barny Butterfield of Sandford Orchards won the Devon County Agricultural Association's John Neason Award in 2016 – he'd already won it before. Barny comes from a non-

Some Devon Cider Makers

ASHRIDGE, Barkingdon Farm, Staverton, Totnes
Jason Mitchell produces organic sparkling vintage cider, plus other drinks.
BERRY FARM CIDER, Axminster
Makes Organic Cider.
BOLLHAYES, near Hemyock, Cullompton
Alex Hill makes farmhouse ciders.
BRIMBLESCOMBE, Farrant's Farm, Dunsford, Exeter
Ron and Beverley Barter make straw-pressed farmhouse cider.
CHUCKLEHEAD, South Hayes Farm, Shillingford, nr Tiverton
Cider using West Country apples.
COUNTRYMAN, Fulldownhead, Milton Abbot, Tavistock
Vernon Shutler produces traditional farmhouse cider, with orchard and shop.
COURTNEYS OF WHIMPLE, Oak Lodge, Southbrook Lane, Whimple, EX5 2PD
Paul and Linda Courtney make Silly Cow cider and juices, and offer orchard services
CREBER'S ROCK, Mammouth Trees, South Brent
Giles Nicholson sells his cider at his farmhouse shop.
GRAY'S FARMHOUSE CIDER, Halston Farm, Tedburn St Mary, Exeter
Ben Gray claims to be fifteenth generation producing farmhouse cider.
GREEN MAN CIDER, Landkey, North Devon
Ben Totterdell and Simon Houghton produce cider and juice at Landkey in North Devon.
GREEN VALLEY CIDER, Dart's Farm, Clyst St George, Exeter
Chris Coles and Nick Pring sell their still, sparkling and fruit cider as well as many other local ciders.
GRIMPSTONELEIGH, Lower Grimpstoneleigh, East Allington, Kingsbridge
Kevin Frost makes vintage cider and juice from his own apples, including Pig's Snout
HANCOCK'S DEVON CIDER, Clapworthy Mill, South Molton
Long-established family firm produces ciders and apple juice.
HERON VALLEY, Crannacombe Farm, Hazelwood, Loddiswell, Kingsbridge
Natasha Green makes cider, cider vinegar, juices and bubbly drinks.

HUNT'S CIDER, Broadleigh Farm, Coombe House Lane, Stoke Gabriel, Totnes
Richard Hunt's family have been making cider at Paignton and now Stoke Gabriel for two hundred years.
INDICKNOWLE FARM, Combe Martin, Ilfracombe
Mark and Sue West make straw pressed cider on family's equipment dating from 1870s.
KENNFORD, Lamacraft Farm, Kennford, Exeter
Straw-pressed farmhouse cider.
KILLERTON, National Trust, Killerton, Exeter
Cider and apple juice from 50 acres of orchards using two-hundred-year-old press.
LUSCOMBE ORGANIC DRINKS, Dean Court, Dean Prior, Buckfastleigh
Gabriel David produces about a score of organic drinks, including Devon cider and 'mostly' Devon apple juice. The label strapline uses the expression 'wild orchards'.
LYME BAY WINERY, Shute, Axminster
Founded by Michael Howard, makes traditional country drinks, including ciders (product names of Jack Ratt and Annings are used), fruit wines, meads, fruit liqueurs and English wines.
MILLTOP ORCHARD, The Mill, Luton, Chudleigh, Newton Abbot
Ann and Peter Webb produce 5000l of apple juice plus 1500l of cider, using apples from Milltop orchards. Also sell fresh fruit.
OSTLERS, Cider Mill, Goodleigh, Barnstaple
Becci Hartnoll making organic cider vinegar (with mother), chutney and scrumpy cider.
REDDAWAY'S FARM CIDER, Lower Rixdale Farm, Luton, Chudleigh, Newton Abbot
Produce traditional farm cider from their own apples. Shop.
SANDFORD ORCHARDS, The Cider Works, Commonmarsh Lane, Crediton
Grown from traditional farm business, now producing juices and ciders for national and international markets. Fruits come from own and rented orchards.
SAMPFORD COURTNEY CIDER, Solland Farm, Sampford Courtney, Okehampton
14,000 trees. Traditional Devon cider and fruit ciders.
SPRYWOOD CROSS, Wooda Farm, Black Torrington, Beaworthy
Russell and Jo Homan use the 'methode champenoise' to produce a sparkling cider.
THOMPSTONE'S DEVONSHIRE CIDER, The Cider Barn, Mitchelcombe Farm, Holne, Tavistock
Andy Thompstone produces traditional hand-pressed cider from Dabinett apples from Holy Park orchard at Mitchelcombe on Dartmoor.
VENTON'S DEVON CYDER, Venton's Cyder Farm, Clyst St Lawrence, Exeter
Mark Venton makes straw-pressed Skippy's scrumpy.
WINKLEIGH CIDER, Wester Barn, Hatherleigh Road, Winkleigh
David Bridgman and partners make traditional ciders, scrumpy and fruit-flavoured ciders on the site of Sam Inch's legendary works, after an unhappy intervention by Bulmer's in the 1990s.
WHIDDON FARM CIDER, The Barn, Lower Whiddon Farm, Ashburton, Newton Abbot
Gerald Vallance makes cider from apples from nearby orchard.
YARDE REAL DEVON CIDER, RealDrink Ltd, Elmcroft Broad Park, Stoke Gabriel
Producing and selling ciders, cordials and juices.

THE DEVON ORCHARDS BOOK

Above: *Pruning for Sandford Orchards, Sandford, near Crediton.* (Paul McLoughlin, www.flickr.com/photos/macdad1948)

Top right: *Sandford Orchards' new trees, Sandford, near Crediton.* (Paul McLoughlin, www.flickr.com/photos/macdad1948)

Right: *Fruit Picking for Sandford Orchards, Sandford, near Crediton.* (Paul McLoughlin, www.flickr.com/photos/macdad1948)

agricultural background in Crediton. He started his family farm business on a Devon County Council small-holding of 75 acres, rearing organic chickens, growing forage, grazing beef cattle and producing cider (for sale in 2003). There were a lot of neglected orchards in his parish, Sandford, (that would have originally served the Creedy Valley Cider factory in Crediton which closed in the 1960s), and Barny collected the fruit. Production was just 1500 litres then, had grown to 12,000 litres in 2010, and 600,000 litres by 2016, generating twelve full-time job equivalents in the process. The brand is Sandford Orchards, and the base is now the Cider Factory in Crediton, back making cider after a period as a fertiliser store. Barny says that the huge commercial operators cannot compete with the craft makers when it comes to provenance and quality. 'If we can all have a morsel of the market that they currently scoff we'll see plenty more orchards on these hills'. But are there sufficient orchards to meet the tremendous increase in production that demand for Barny's cider has achieved? Pressing fresh fruit is one of Barny's key criteria for a craft cider. His advertisements say 'Our fertile corner of Devon is the perfect place to grow cider apples; that is why every apple that goes into our Red Cider is grown within 30 miles of our press'.

REVIVAL AND THE FUTURE

Winkleigh Cider has inherited the site of Sam Inch's plant which was taken on (and then closed) by Bulmers in 1999. So cider has been made under three names, but David Bridgman has been there throughout and has ensured continuity of supply from orchards. Sam Inch took apples from local growers, and although Bulmers planted an orchard next to the factory this was sold on, so the firm doesn't have its own domestic supply. Most years Winkleigh Cider will takes apples from about fifteen local farm orchards and a few specialist orchards. Occasionally, when the crop is poor, they look outside the county as far as Herefordshire. They like the local grower because of 'lovely varieties', but the variable harvest is a challenge and indeed the number of orchards that supply them is diminishing. Because of better management the specialist orchards are more reliable. Some of the 'gentlemen's agreements' with smaller producers go back a long way, so the company doesn't want to abandon them. The reality is that for most of the smaller growers their orchards are less important than other farm activities so they become neglected and unreliable to the user. The specialist grower has invested a lot in his orchards so needs more reliable purchasers, and will understandably press for a contract.

Green Valley, based at out-of-town shopping complex Dart's Farm (near Topsham) is named after the Clyst Valley. It has been called Whiteway's Phoenix by James Crowden because its owners (Chris Coles and Nick Pring), their craft and equipment (originally 5000 gallon vats) all moved to Dart's Farm when Whiteway's closed. They brought with them their apple suppliers, from Whimple itself and also Butterleigh, Kenton, Newton Poppleford, Silverton and Woodbury Salterton. Green Valley has established itself as a beacon for craft made ciders and juices from around the county.

Tremlett's Bitter (red) and White Close Pippin (yellow) at Combe Martin. (Tim Potter)

Apple Picking, Venn, Landkey – Ben and Simon of Green Man Cider and their dogs. (All Tim Potter)

Bee hives in orchard, Whimple.

Sheep at Solland Farm, home of Sampford Courtney Cider.

Orchards Serving On-Farm Cider Makers

It is not easy to obtain an overview of cider-drinking in Devon and how it relates to orchards. How much is drunk? What proportion comes from Devon producers, and what proportion of them are using the products of Devon orchards? The Devon Branch of CAMRA has produced A Guide to Devon ciders and where they can be found, but the information is self-admittedly not always up to date. UK Cider is not much better; it lists pubs (and a few shops) where cider can be obtained, but there seems to be no evidence of a systematic survey, and again information is sometimes so lamentably out of date that it becomes erroneous. So the attempt to produce an overview is further complicated by the definitional problem of what constitutes a Devon cider both in terms of content and the way it is made. The Devon Cyder Guild are aware of the issues, and there are valid contradictory arguments.

On-farm cider makers are almost exclusively taking advantage of duty exemptions and keeping within the production limits given above, but how many there are varies from year to year and is unknown. However, the orchards needed to serve them are not substantial; usually their own plus a few others, particularly in years when apples are in short supply. Regularity of supply and consistency of product become issues when the apple supply is uncertain.

It is not as easy as it was to find outlets for on-farm cider. If offering cider for sale, the maker, the premises and the product have to conform with regulations. There are still sales at the farmhouse gate, but these are diminishing, as are outlets at pubs and shops. Long gone are most cider-only pubs, originally called cider houses, when they were a room in a house or cottage selling the locally made drink. Ye Olde Mason's Arms at Branscombe was a cider house with a bar 8ftx4ft but many cider houses would not have a bar at all. Today locally made cider farmhouse cider made from known apple varieties from local orchards and available for local consumption is becoming a rare experience.

THE DEVON ORCHARDS BOOK

Vernon and Theresa Shutler harvesting apples, Felldownhead, Milton Abbot.

Apple silo and hoist, Countryman Cider, Felldownhead, Milton Abbot.

Vernon Shutler loads pressed apple cheese – much loved by pigs and cattle.

Mark and Sue West collecting apples, Indicknowle, Combe Martin.

Courtney family collecting apples, Whimple.

Michael Archibald inspects his hive under Tremlett's Bitter at Little Burne Farm, Bickleigh. (Tim Archibald)

Orchards For Home Consumption

Throughout the book there has been mention of the huge number of tiny orchards in towns and villages and scattered across the Devon countryside, all producing apples for home consumption. In most senses it has never been easier to establish your own orchard. 'Grow Your Own' has become a popular slogan. The availability of trees in terms of variety and size would astound past generations. There is advice on growing everywhere. There are easy opportunities to make drinks thanks to the ready availability of equipment designed for domestic use. However, setting aside the fact that most people do not wish to 'grow their own' given the readily availability of prepared food and drink, there is one huge challenge to orchards for domestic use – the availability of land, and essentially the price of land. This works two ways. First, many existing domestic orchards in towns and villages are vulnerable because they are valuable as building sites – their limited protection was mentioned earlier. Second, the density of many new housing developments restricts the opportunities for garden orchards.

Nevertheless, orchards for home consumption are still around in abundance. Nurseryman Kevin Croucher has noted a subtle shift in demand for trees influenced by the 'Grow Your Own' campaigns. An example is given of an allotment orchard at Torrington – an example of how orchard enthusiasm can overcome the challenge of land availability.

REVIVAL AND THE FUTURE

Orchard at Pippacott, Braunton, with Tony and Anne Featherstone.

Chris Niesigh demonstrates equipment on a cider making course. (Tim Potter)

An Allotment Orchard at Torrington.

Sheena and John Pledger have developed an orchard on a Great Torrington Town Council allotment on a steep-sloping south-facing site, north of the town. A remarkably imaginative variety of trees has been assembled. The orchard developed up the slope, so starting at the bottom is a collection of dessert and cooking apples on M 106 rootstock. Next comes an 'orchard garden' of bush and espalier trees – home-grown seedlings (some named after family members) and West Country apples. Further up is a collection of pears, then plums and finally cider apples. The orchard is appealing to the eye; the events associated with it, particularly harvest-time, bring together the family, friends and other allotment holders.

New garden planting at Croyde. (Tim Potter)

THE DEVON ORCHARDS BOOK

Standard trees, produced by John Worle in Herefordshire.

Orchards Where Fruit Production Is Less Important

Ironically, just as orchard acreage in Devon and nationwide was increasing, so there suddenly emerged a concern for the disappearance of orchards. While the increase was mostly in what some would call plantations of bush trees, the decline was of traditional orchards, which were clearly no longer 'economic'. The hunt was on for other uses.

Common Ground's campaign to save (traditional) orchards caught the public imagination. Essentially what it did was to redefine them; they became ends in themselves rather than as means of fruit production. Or rather, in some cases, they became means to other ends than fruit production. Chapter Ten was devoted to our orchard heritage and probably would never have been written without the mental shift that has occurred.

Nationally orchards now have recognition as being far more than fruit production. There is an Orchard Network of major organisations that are working together to ensure that our orchard heritage, and particularly biodiversity, is recognised and conserved.

In Devon there is a lot of activity with no formal Network, but there is networking. Organisations work

THORNHAYES

Looking back a generation ago to the 1980s there was a very limited supply of 'traditional' West Country apple varieties from local nurseries. In commercial horticulture there was a tendency to see a future of a limited number of new varieties, supported by a system of sprays etc to overcome local disadvantages.

Kevin Croucher was a Lecturer in Horticulture at Bicton College. 'Local varieties were despised and many introductions were not suited to wet climate or soils' he says. Mid-century Duncan Metford, College Fruit Officer, had established bush orchards and trial orchards of cider varieties and Kevin developed an interest in their performance.

In 1990 Kevin bought 7 acres of grassland at Dulford near Cullompton and set up Thornhayes Nursery. His intention was to grow garden ornamental stock with a few orchard trees. He acquired a collection of old varieties from Scotts of Merriot in Somerset. He sold around just 200 trees in 1991. With the launch of Save our Orchards, Apple Days and Devon CC grants he was able to meet a need for local varieties in a dearth of supply. He doubled production every year for the best part of the 1990s decade until he was producing 3000-4000 trees per year. People brought him varieties so his stock collection grew to 250 trees.

Kevin Croucher with his stock collection of Devon varieties, Thornhayes Nursery.

REVIVAL AND THE FUTURE

Field grafting, Adam's Apples, Talaton.

Orchard tree nursery, Adam's Apples, Talaton.

Field grafting, Adam's Apples, Talaton.

> ### ORCHARD LINK, ORCHARDS LIVE AND TAVY AND TAMAR APPLE GROUP
>
> There are three organisations providing advice and other services covering substantial parts of the county – Orchard Link (northern Devon), Orchards Live ('greater' South Hams) and the Tavy and Tamar Apple Group. Up-to-date information on all three groups can be found on their websites, so only a brief word on their origins and operational differences is required here.
>
> ORCHARD LINK has a name which reflects the original (1990s) prime function, to link the growers of fruit with users. Originally a telephone service, it persists as the useful 'Harvestline'. At the time of its origin the South Hams District Council and the South Devon AONB were involved in orchard work – advising, demonstrating and conserving local varieties. It was only as this work diminished that there became a place for Orchard Link to morph into the role of the volunteer-run, not-for-profit organisation that it performs today.
>
> The five purposes can be summarised as: technical advice on restoration and planting, conservation of local fruit varieties, productive use (through hire of equipment and 'Harvestline'), exchange of skills and expertise, and community involvement.
>
> ORCHARDS LIVE describes itself as a group of enthusiasts who are reversing the decline of standard orchards in the northern half of the county. It is an activity of the Dartington North Devon Charitable Trust with its own advisory committee.
>
> Its origins can be traced to 1991 as a response to Common Ground's Save our Orchards Campaign linked to their poignant photographs of orchard decline commissioned from James Ravilious. It has been remarkably successful considering its operation in the part of the county with fewest orchards. Membership was initially free, and has remained low, attracting a membership of around two hundred.
>
> A booklet celebrating its twentieth birthday listed six themes, including raising public awareness, practical help through the loan of equipment, co-operation with other bodies, and the sixth theme was the vision which underpinned everything else.
>
> The TAVY AND TAMAR APPLE GROUP is a not-for-profit association based on the Bere Peninsula. It was established in 2009. Its objective is to encourage the rejuvenation of local orchards through best practice and sustainable management. Its aspiration is the availability of local apples in supermarkets across the region. The subscription is £5 per year, and there are over a hundred members.
>
> The Group offers training events, a very successful Autumn AppleFest and an annual Wassail. The special characteristic from the start has been the emphasis on equipment, and there is now a full range of equipment for hire at attractive rates, with trained operators to oversee use.
>
> The success of all three groups is a remarkable achievement given the limited experience and resources with which they started. Quite new forms of orchard activity are proving resilient.

together on projects. Perhaps a loose forum might emerge? Events and ready exchanges of information can be a great stimulus.

One significant result of the realisation of the environmental importance of orchards has been their inclusion in the Countryside Stewardship funding scheme. The objects of Countryside Stewardship are the protection and enhancement of the natural environment – in particular the diversity of wildlife. Natural England are charged with assessing habitats for conservation, and they have done this by dividing the county into zones with different environmental priorities. Across much of the county remnants of traditional orchards which receive favourable appraisals can be 'maintained', while on the Devon Redlands (in the east) are there also funds for restoration. The Scheme has worthy intentions, but by evaluating

REVIVAL AND THE FUTURE

Memorial orchard trees, Cockington.

existing rather than potential environmental features it tends to perpetuate existing orchard sites rather than encourage new ones. Was the Scheme modelled on grants for woodland restoration? Orchards require considerable management in their early years, and there is not always evidence of this. The second point is that there is little evidence of how replanted trees will be used; traditional standard orchards produced a crop, and the crop usually paid for the management. The Scheme claims 'If successful there will be a well-managed traditional orchard with a range of healthy young and old trees. This includes established grass, tall bushy hedges, scrub and tall herb vegetation with abundancy of invertebrates, birds and wildflowers.' A successful scheme in my North Devon parish, with thorough formative pruning, already produces tons of apples for a new local cider maker. However, another established cider maker was unaware of any new fruit coming his way from the Scheme; a local farmer had planted seventy replacement trees, but claimed he did not know how to prune them.

The National Trust undertook a nationwide overview of it orchards in 2007. While the Trust had played a significant role in establishing the national Orchard Network, the review revealed a remarkably low number on Trust properties.

The Royal Horticultural Society Garden at Rosemoor, near Torrington, has developed since 1988 when Lady Anne Berry donated her garden. I remember proposing the first Apple Day in Devon to a welcoming but apprehensive staff. Apprehension was soon swept away by the Garden's first daily attendance of over 1000, and the Day soon became an annual event. Now, a quarter of a century later, the collection of trees in and around the Vegetable Garden has been complemented by a new orchard of 45 mostly Devon varieties grafted on to 'robust'(M116) rootstocks, designed to grow in to wide canopied trees. Underneath will be a meadow for the public to explore and for wildlife to flourish.

The People's Trust for Endeangered Species (PTES) has identified about fifty Community Orchards in the county, and this considerably underrepresents the number there are because many are not very effective in promoting themselves. New ones are emerging all the time. A visit to PTES's website not only produces a list but information on the nearest ones. What is a Community Orchard? Common Ground must be credited for promoting the concept. A community orchard, they said, can

- help conserve local varieties of fruit
- contribute to the beauty and distinctiveness of your locality
- provide an attractive place for walking, picnicking and relaxation
- be a focus for community activity
- provide a source of fresh fruit for local people
- attract wildlife – birds, insects and wildflowers.

Interestingly the concept and the first examples included existing orchards such as Lustleigh on the edge of Dartmoor, where community use already existed. But early on orchards were planted, such as the Millennium Green at Landkey. Recently most new community orchards are ones that have been planted. This makes it difficult to achieve some of the objects listed above immediately.

Growing Community Orchards was a Heritage Lottery funded project in south Devon in 2016 and 2017. It was a partnership between Orchard Link and South Devon Area of Outstanding Natural Beauty, involving an impressive total of 23 community orchards. The broad case for the Project was argued twofold. First there was the loss of 90% of Devon's orchards since the 1950s and the need to safeguard remaining ones through working with voluntary community groups, and second there was the gaining of support through engaging the wider communities. The Project had a fourfold thrust:

-giving groups skills and expertise to manage sites,
-helping groups develop,
-creating a network of skills and experience,
-create a community orchards website.

The final report has impressive statistics. 23 groups were

LANDKEY MILLENNIUM GREEN

Planted in December 1999, Landkey has one of the last orchards of the last Millennium. It is an orchard of mazzard trees, traditionally called 'greens' or 'gardens', so it will be referred to as a green. Mazzards are small black cherries, once common, but recently restricted almost exclusively to a small part of North Devon, east of Barnstaple. Their distinctiveness provided the inspiration for a unique public open space.

Landkey has its unique Green for three main reasons: the vision of a few, the wholehearted support of many and a number of fortuitous and timely opportunities.

The main visionary was Dick Joy, Parish Council Chairman for many years. Dick was reared with a strong understanding of the parish's agricultural traditions. He remembered the marvels of blossom time, 'like going to Heaven', the fruit's distinct flavour, and had many amusing anecdotes. Determined that mazzards should not disappear, in the 1970s he encouraged local nurseryman Fred Harris to produce trees. Graft wood from Walter King but was not easily obtained from high, ancient trees, 'like getting grandparents to breed'. New trees found homes in gardens and orchards, but there was no planting of a distinct mazzard green.

The wholehearted support of many came to be demonstrated by two projects which had their origins in Common Ground's promotion of locality and common culture. Dartington's Save our Orchards campaign aimed to re-establish a mazzard green and organised a seminar. There was a Local Distinctiveness project in which Landkey villagers discussed a new green, but no site was readily available, although Kevin Croucher of Thornhayes Nursery had started producing young trees.

The opportunities which enabled vision and support to become reality were a planning decision and the Millennium. A 1996 Planning Inquiry had declared a field near the heart of the village as unsuitable for housing. The new National Lottery provided funds for Millennium projects; these included new village greens. Land was generously given to Landkey Parish Council, to be divided between public amenity (Millennium Green) and Football Club uses. A major feature of the Millennium Green would be 65 large mazzard trees, covering over 2 acres.

Lottery funding had to be matched, but donation of the land, complemented by free site preparation works (under-grounding of overhead cables and pedestrian bridge works) meant that fund-raising was not a problem. By December 1999 the site was ready for its pot-grown trees, planted by young people with their parents. Trees of five varieties (Bottler, Dun, Greenstem Black, Small Black and later Hannaford) on Colt rootstock were planted with staggered spacing at 35 feet apart. Lottery rules determined the form and nature of the Green, and the modern variants on a traditional mazzard green were the footpath, seats, interpretive panel (later joined by a notice board) and machine-cut (rather than sheep-grazed) sward. The Green was opened formally in July 2000.

The trees have flourished, (with no predicted vandalism), and with formative pruning have grown well. The trees take two decades or more to reach maturity, and although Colt is

Landkey Millennium Green; entrance to mazzard green.

described as a 'reducing' rootstock the trees are reaching 20 feet in height. The exposed nature of the site means lateral branches on the leeward side are growing strongest, and the vision of branches meeting may have to wait. Some varieties have grown faster than others. Blossom is splendid, if tantalisingly unpredictable, most springs. In 2015 there was a huge fruit crop, quite defeating birds, so Landkey residents could pick and eat mazzards – many for the first time. The fruit did not always match the varieties' expected shapes, size and flavours, raising questions about nomenclature, and genetic testing has started.

Trustees and volunteers maintain and safeguard the Green at ridiculously low cost; it is a credit to them. Alongside the mazzards the Green also includes a new copse, open grassland, a small apple orchard, and the Tarka Trail footpath beside the stream. It is used for community events, and in 2016 a survey revealed that over two hundred people per day visit the Green with high levels of satisfaction.

Mazzards (twelve years old) blooming on Landkey Millennium Green, May 2012.

involved, although it is admitted that not all groups fully 'showed up'. 317 people attended a total of 23 training workshops (some people attended more than once making a total of 551 attendances). 3784 days were given by participants and volunteers. Stronger engagement with the local orchard conservation body, Orchard Link, didn't materialise as hoped, but there were three significant outcomes. First, the Project had expanded the capacity of some groups and acted as a real catalyst for change. Second, orchards are being more skilfully and effectively cared for, with ongoing management plans and higher levels of community support. Third, Orchard Link has a new sense of purpose and direction.

Community Orchards, a concept of the 1990s, are alive and still growing three decades later. The quote from Charlotte of Modbury at the end sums up the success of the Project: 'We now have a use for the apples grown in the community orchard and provide a pressing service for apples brought in for community use. There is a better awareness of the orchard and apples. The Wassail got people to the orchard who might not normally go. The Wassail has introduced a great community event and gathering in an unusual time of year. And the public has been tasting REAL apple juice and loving it'

The Project has been both radical and conservative. While the idea of the community managing land in a complicated way is quite radical, the Project's strength has been on reinforcing what is there – both groups and orchards. More radical proposals are under consideration for Exeter and will be considered in the next chapter.

There is a full list of the Project Orchards, and other Community Orchards in Devon in the Box.

It seems appropriate to end this review of the revival of Devon's orchards with Community Orchards because in a sense most of Devon's orchards through history have been communal. Our last chapter will look further ahead.

COMMUNITY ORCHARDS IN DEVON

There is a long-standing tradition of communal access to orchards – manifested in the wassailing tradition. In certain places orchards have been used for other events, such as Town Orchard at Lustleigh on Dartmoor with its popular annual MayDay Festival. In a few places orchards have become the property of the local community and are owned by the Parish Council (as at Bickleigh).

Over the last few decades there has been an explosion of interest in Community Orchards. In 1989 Common Ground produced a book *Orchards, A Guide to Local Conservation* which mentioned scope for community conservation, with Lustleigh as an example. With interest in orchard conservation across the nation many local groups, schools, wildlife organisations and local authorities wanted to adopt or establish their own orchards, and these became known as community orchards. In 2011 Common Ground published a *Guide to Community Orchards*. 'It shows groups and individuals how to start their own community orchard, from gathering support, tackling legal issues and access, to organising working parties and selling produce. It gives suggestions on "apple mapping" and saving local varieties, and of course it gives practical advice on planting, harvesting and safeguarding your orchard.'

The Landkey Millennium Green which incorporates an orchard of 65 mazzard trees is described in a separate Box. The model which has worked at Landkey is the availability of a good site, a good 'story' of local fruit, generous public funding for establishment, support from the local community (including politicians) and a good group of local volunteers. It isn't always like this, and few of the other community orchards in North Devon press all the buttons. At South Molton there have been

THE DEVON ORCHARDS BOOK

Widening community support: 'Growing Orchard Communities' event.

drainage problems, Hele at Ilfracombe is on a steep slope, Hatherleigh is across the by-pass away from the town. Most Community Orchards in North Devon are on Council-owned land, and some are what might be called 'problematical pieces' – things which can be a deterrent to successful community 'ownership'. An interesting concept is the development of linear orchards along the Tarka Trail, a former railway line which has been converted into a cycle way and footpath. Lateral orchard groves for visitors to appreciate is a lovely idea, but which community will make long-term commitment if the best fruit is to be snatched by cyclists; no volunteer corps for cores! Efforts to bring together the dozen or more community orchards in North Devon have so far been only partially successful.

South Devon provides a very different story. The 'Growing Community Orchards' run by the South Devon Area of Outstanding Natural Beauty working with Orchards Link has now wound up. It involved community orchards in an area that stretches from Plymouth to Torquay.

There are about half a dozen community orchards in Plymouth, several in and around Exeter, and others in the eastern part of the county.

PROVISIONAL LIST

There is a list on the People's Trust for Endangered Species (PTES) website. This includes some that don't appear there:

Ashburton, Beeson, Broadclyst, Bishopsteignton, Chillington, Cockington, Colwell Woods, Cornwood & Lutton, Cornworthy, Cowick Barton Playing Fields (Exeter), Dartmouth, Foxhole (Dartington), Follaton Arboretum (Totnes), Follaton Cemetery (Totnes), Fremington, Halberton, Hatherleigh, Hemersdon, Hele (Ilfracombe), Hillsborough, Holberton, Holcombe, Honiton. Huxham's Cross (Dartington), Instow, Killerton, Lagoon (Yelland), Littleham, Lower Sharpham Barton, Ludwell Valley (Exeteer), Lupton, Lustleigh, MacAndrew's Field, Mincinglake Valley Park, Modbury, Newton & Noss, Plymouth (x7), Ringmoor, St George's Avenue, Sandford Millennium Green, Sid Meadow, South Molton, Sparkwell, Stokenham, Weare Gifford, Week, Wembury, Whimple, Woodbury, Yeo Valley.

Opposite: *Training Day for 'Growing Orchard Communities' project.*

REVIVAL AND THE FUTURE

Following the PTES Orchard Survey in Clyst Valley near Exeter.

Ch 12
The Future

In the 1520s would the monks have been able to predict what was to happen to their orchards just a decade later? More recently, who could have predicted that Bulmers would have overseas owners? Likewise, when the Save our Orchards Campaigns were established in the 1990s, who could have predicted the numbers of Apple Festivals and Community Orchards there are now? Predicting the future of orchards is fraught! In looking ahead I have grouped issues under the headings of social, commercial, environmental and political. I then draw the issues together and conclude with my personal aspirations.

Social

In talking to all sectors of orchard owners I have been struck by a general confidence in the future. 'Grow Local, Eat and Drink Local', was a catch phrase that received frequent mentions. Orchards are wanted, and if one accepts that half the battle to achieve anything is conviction, then the battle to safeguard orchards is being won.

As the world shrinks so the pride in local identity has grown. There's ambivalence because people want universality and localness at the same time, but perhaps that's no bad thing? Devon may not have an apple on its road signs like Herefordshire, but orchards and their products are seen as part of the county's identity, and a growing number of people are working to ensure they remain so.

The image of cider is key. 'Demand Devon Cider' says the advert of Sandford Orchards. The county's product may not always have had the best reputation, but many of the county's cider and juice makers are working to drive up quality. Orchards will be sustained by cider of good quality.

'Grow your Own' and 'Five a Day' campaigns have led to increased demand for fruit, with enlightened employers supplying fruit for their workers. Schools may be championing fruit, but bright red apples prevail over local varieties. Will this recognition of the benefits of fruit eventually benefit Devon's orchards? There are not many fruit farms in the county to supply dessert or culinary fruit,

Vigo

Vigo is mentioned because its history reflects the way that fruit processing has changed and developed over the last three decades, and that tells us a lot about orchards.

Vigo was established in London in 1981 after Alex Hill had spotted a fruit press when on holiday in Hungary. He soon saw there was UK demand, so he imported more. He moved Vigo from a railway arch in London to Dunkeswell in 1987 and watched his firm grow and grow until employing more than twenty skilled people. Alex's retirement brought changes.

VIGO PRESSES sells a range of crushers/mills, presses, pasteurisers and other kit within the pockets and technical capabilities of smaller producers. It has both reflected and enabled a surge in small-scale and domestic juice and cider production.

VIGO Ltd focusses on the needs of the commercial cider makers and juice producers. It also provides brewery equipment, winemaking equipment and vineyard supplies.

and very few Devonians would know what local fruits to ask for. Some may resent the dominance of certain non-Devon varieties like Cox or Bramley, but has any effort been put into marketing Devon varieties effectively?

The relict farm orchards are getting smaller in number. The number of farmers who gather the fruit and take it to the local cider maker is getting smaller too. Yet many makers will say that it is their knowledge of local varieties that creates a unique product. Some are already being forced to use the same apples varieties as volume makers; the practice undermines the whole concept of localness. Secondly, still-productive old orchards can provide the 'way in' for new drink makers by providing a cheap, but hand-picked, raw material. Cut out these innovators and you've reduced the 'spread' of makers and products, and thereby the success stories of the future.

The enthusiasm for establishing Community Orchards has yet to impress those looking for both sound management and significant fruit production, but perhaps that's not the point. The success of 'Growing Orchards Communities' in the South Hams may be an indicator of what's to come. We should recognise the importance of informal social arrangements such as the harroldcalvados.com who harvest at Whimple. Social media allows new groups to develop fast.

Political

Government policy can affect orchards directly and indirectly – for example directly through grants to plant (or grub up), or indirectly through duty on cider. The current issue facing agriculture is BREXIT and its consequences. First, there is withdrawal from the Common Agricultural Policy (CAP) and the substantial support for agriculture which flowed from it. The reform of the CAP has been under discussion for some time. The words which emerged at 2018's Oxford Farming Conference were 'public good'; any new farm grants would have to demonstrate 'public good' benefits. What case for orchards could emerge? Will environmental projects such as Stewardship Schemes be continued? Uncertainties also apply to EU regional grant replacements. Second the possible end of free movement of

Orchard replanting (middle distance) Colyton.

THE FUTURE

Stewardship

Originating under a different name in the 1990s, Countryside Stewardship provides funding for farmers (and others) to make environmental improvements. The scheme is competitive, and there are local priority targets.

The qualification criteria are quite complex, but many farmers with orchards in Devon have qualified under past schemes, and traditional orchards can receive support under the present one. The scheme claims 'If successful there will be a well-managed traditional orchard with a range of healthy young and old trees. This includes established grass, tall bushy hedges, scrub and tall herb vegetation with abundancy of invertebrates, birds and wildflowers.' There are three reasons for its mention here. First its scale, because it has attracted many participants. Second, the funding is significant. Third is the support the creation or management of traditional orchards. Having been involved with a successful scheme in my parish I can sing Stewardship's praises, but anecdotal evidence is perhaps not the best way to obtain a comprehensive picture, and not every scheme has had subsequent success. Unfortunately orchard-specific data for Devon are not readily available: at some stage there should be an informed review of the scheme's operation.

Neglected new planting near Hartland. (Tim Potter)

labour is a concern across the horticultural industry, but it an issue in other counties more than Devon. Third, if patterns of trade are going to change substantially how might they affect Devon growers and the market for fruit and drinks?

A longer term political issue is the relationship between agriculture, food, drink and health. An assured supply of food and regulation of the quality of food have always been seen as political issues, but the abuse of their diet by the public is more problematical. Duties on alcohol were originally a simple revenue matter, but no longer; there has always been a concession to the farming industry in allowing small-scale production, but could abuse of alcohol lead to changes? It is high-alcohol 'white cider' that is the present target, but ironically changes of duty may also concern higher alcohol craft cider makers.

Commercial

Commercial and financial considerations are huge determinants of Devon's larger orchards. Nationwide cider sales have been a huge commercial success, rising for decades, with plateaus or small falls before another rise. However, the overall picture can disguise changes in the component parts such as nature of demand, the ways in which cider is supplied and the ways clever entrepreneurs deal with these changes. So forecasters look to market sectors for winners and losers; which brands are strong, will provenance remain a strong selling point, and will a return to 'authenticity' replace fruit-flavoured ciders? There are cider brands from Cornwall, Devon and Somerset that were little known two decades ago which all use Devon's apples. Provenance is important, and it is up to those who market cider to promote it to their advantage. As for 'authenticity', tastes are fickle, but they are there to be cultivated.

Against this background what are the chances of newcomers planting a large commercial orchard? There are the costs of land, planting, no significant immediate return, and perhaps £100,000 for new equipment. Herefordshire has been the most favoured county, and new contract plantings the most favoured route, but contract plantings on an overall modest scale have done well in Devon too. Cider makers in other counties are unlikely to establish contracts involving a long haul of fruit, but expanding Devon cider makers will look for local supply.

Environmental

Climate change is the big issue which is having an impact on orchards all over the world. In Herefordshire some cider trees are flowering a week earlier than usual. Three aspects of change have already been noted and are predicted to continue in Devon; more variable or violent weather, the rise in winter temperatures and heat/drought stress in summer.

Adjustments to climate change can be made and some

Fullabrook Wind Farm turbine above orchard at Pippacott, Braunton.

> **NATIONAL TRUST**
>
> The National Trust undertook a nationwide audit of orchards in 2008. This identified orchards at a score of Devon properties, but a significant area at only one: Killerton. (Killerton now holds a very large Apple Day in Sparrow Park Orchard.) Management may be as part of a garden, as part of the wider countryside and managed by a countryside service, or as part of a farm tenancy. There have been a number of projects involving restoration or replanting, particularly around 2008 and '09 as part of the Orchards Network initiative with Natural England.
>
> Valuable work has been undertaken by the Trust's Plant Conservation Centre (for the whole country) which happens to be based at Talaton, east of Exeter.

studies suggest that there might be new opportunities. At the moment there is no dramatic action, and perhaps that is the way it will remain? If climate change requires planting of new varieties this will be easier because of the shorter life of most trees in commercial orchards. Climate change will be more of a challenge to standard orchards of long-lived trees of traditional varieties.

We have seen that the importance of traditional orchards for wildlife has received rather late recognition. There is therefore not a long track record of orchard conservation work by bodies like the Devon Wildlife Trust, the National Trust and the National Parks. There are now changed attitudes and more focus, and this can be expected to continue and grow, particularly as organisations gain experience in management.

Regulations restricting the use of many insecticides and herbicides, and increasing costs, have led to a more targeted approach amongst orchard owners, and this will continue.

A visit to Dartington prompted new thoughts. The Agroforestry Research Trust some time ago introduced agroforestry to Dartington. Nearby Schumacher College is championing sustainability. One has its forest garden, the other its Schumacher gardens. Nearby the Dartington Estate

THE FUTURE

Left: *Schumacher College's 'orchard', Dartington.*

Below: *New 'silvo-arable' planting, including Elder and Sichuan Peppers at Broadlears, Dartington.*

Author's netted mazzards on GV rootstock, Harford, Landkey.

Waiting for the rush at Killerton Apple Day, 2017.

has established a 48 acre 'silvoarable' area of apples and elder interspersed with other crops. All are concerned with fruit production, and so all have planted fruit trees, but none has planted orchards. They are challenging 'monocultural' orchard thinking and should be watched.

Traditional orchards also have importance as landscape and recreational features, but their planting or conservation on these grounds is still novel but likely to increase.

Vision For The Future

Devon's orchard fruit products should be easily available. This is more easily said than done with the closure of pubs and greengrocers. Occasional farmers' markets are no substitute for supermarkets, but changes in warehousing and distribution are making it much easier for supermarkets to stock local products and, if pressed, can respond.

There are many models of communities and individuals growing their own food, often alongside those who don't, and orchards can be a part of this. This can be done individually if one has a garden or allotment. A lovely example is the allotment orchard of Sheena and John Pledger with a remarkable collection of Devon varieties and seedlings on small trees. By contrast Jane Pay has pursued top grafting to produce different varieties on one tree – an attractive practice which is remarkably unpursued. Such activities are not practicable for everybody. Corporate fruit growing on allotments, in community orchards or through adoption of trees in gardens has worked in other places and is gaining a foothold in Devon.

There should be easier access to orchards such as open days and more community orchards, and they should work together more effectively to promote themselves. In the 1990s I suggested that every community should have an

> **EXE RIVERSIDE**
>
> There are a number of projects involving new orchards around Exeter, such as Ide, Cranbrook Country Park and Exe Riverside Valley Park. These build on a number of established community orchards and projects such as Mincinglake Valley Park. An Exeter and East Devon Green Infrastructure Strategy, with a Manager and office at Cranbrook, opens up interesting possibilities for the future
>
> The Valley Park which stretches from Exewick to Countess Wear to the west of the city is considered Exeter's premier breathing space. A Master Plan for the Park was adopted by Exeter City Council in 2016, and this includes new orchards. The City, Environment Agency, Devon Wildlife Trust, Arts Council and others are all involved in the implementation of the plan.
>
> A novel aspect are fruit routes, loosely based on work at Loughborough University with environmental artist Anne-Marie Culhane. There 141 identifiable trees (54 varieties), have been planted, with hedgerow trees on a kilometre-long route. Most trees are in six small orchards. The Fruit Route is seen as a base for community activities; as the trees grow there will be foraging, harvesting, eating, cider making and celebration.

> **PTES**
>
> Since 2006 the People's Trust for Endangered Species (PTES) has analysed aerial photographs to identify traditional orchards. Ongoing ground surveys using volunteers show 9% of English orchards are in excellent condition, 45% in good condition and 46% in poor condition. Maps of all orchards and survey results are available on the PTES website. This is a valuable resource which should be more widely known and used.
>
> Anybody wanting to undertake a quick survey of their parish's orchard history and condition could do no better than looking at Dean Milles's responses (South West Heritage Trust), Devon History Society's Orchard Project (for tithe apportionments) and the PTES Survey.

orchard. Is that too impossible an aspiration? We are nearer achieving it than we were in 1990, so let it remain a vision.

In areas of special countryside and around our settlements we should see the landscape value of fruit trees. Could Stewardship Schemes be modified to enable planting in the interest of amenity? So might the orchard component of the Exeter Valley Project be the forerunner of something bigger?

There should be better understanding of orchards and more love of orchards. A starting point for a Parish Orchard Survey is outlined in the PTES Box.

Championing Orchards

It is too easy to advocate the above without suggesting how this vision might be realised. It would be nice if there was an impartial national champion of orchards, but bodies, whether the National Association of Cidermakers, Orchards Network, the Worshipful Company of Fruiterers or others, have constructive interests but partial ones. Common Ground deserve praise for starting a campaign, but no national body resulted. This puts a big responsibility on local champions, but even at Devon county level there is a void.

Why is the story of Devon's orchards promoted so modestly? The success of Apple Days and associated media coverage is an achievement, but there is scope for more. Why has Devon such a small amount of county-wide literature, such as Somerset's Guide to Orchards and Cider Makers, or Herefordshire's Wildlife Friendly Orchards? And if such leaflets exist, but have passed me by, that reinforces my point!

We are told that research and development underpin any successful economic or social initiative, and yet so many research, technical advice, educational and training services that were available a few decades ago have disappeared. I find this a most depressing aspect of the work for this book. If there were to be an assured future for orchards in the county there would be a chapter and not just this paragraph.

However, the availability of information has been transformed thanks to new media and there are still 'traditional' sources such as consultants and courses. New

Bill Wakeham lives on in Cockington Memorial Orchard.
(Peter Rodd)

apple varieties are being trialled and planted. There is remarkable new equipment for the harvesting and processing fruit, and ingenious and effective schemes to use it efficiently.

Although there is a lot of noise from the retailing industry about localness and provenance there is a lot to be done before Devonians can have easy access to local orchard products. 'Local' to supermarkets means 'regional', and distribution systems and scales of operation can't really handle localness. Agreement on provenance is a challenge, as the Devon Cyder Makers Guild has discovered.

Individual Response

It is easier to preach to others than to reform one's own behaviour. I end with a few short suggestions on how the actions of individuals can be transformative. You might make them individual resolutions…

First, orchards are about production, so why not make sure you use or purchase the products? I mostly use my own apples from September to the spring, and although I cannot claim exclusivity in purchasing Devon products I usually have local Devon apple juice and cider in the house, occasionally supported by purchases of fruit to complement what I grow myself. When out for a drink ask for Devon products. Does your local pub pay enough attention to the range and provenance of the drinks it serves?

Second, if you are aware of Orchard events such as walks or Apple Days give them support for a few hours each year. You might obtain that supply of fruit or juice to realise your first resolution.

Third, participate in one of the national surveys or projects, or find a local group such as a Community Orchard and offer help.

Fourth, tell. People want more information. The queues for help with apple identification at Apple Days are often long. People want to hear about the subject; I give talks, and the Vote of Thanks at one could be summarised as 'Much more interesting than our expectations'.

Fifth, plant. In my retirement I planted an orchard of my own. This book is not a manual on orchard establishment, but just to whet appetites there are short appendices.

Conclusion

Has it all been circular? From a county with relatively few orchards through a few centuries when the county was covered with them back to a state where there are fewer orchards, but those are respected and in a few cases revered. In this book I have tried to explain this story, but there's an underlying uncertainty. There's still research to be done on why Devonians took to orchards in such a big way; I understand why they abandoned many of them, and I hope I've explained why they won't disappear altogether.

We have concluded our formal account of Devon's Orchards. We early on talked about the word 'orchard' and how the meaning of the word had evolved. It strikes me that more than ever it is an inadequate word because it is used to describe such a range of land uses. Diversity must be a thought that crosses our mind in looking to the future. This book should have shown that Devon's route to the present position has been a distinctive one; the orchards of the county will retain their diverse characteristics and will find new ones.

Appendix 1
So You Are Thinking of Planting or Restoring a Standard Orchard?

So you are thinking of planting or restoring a standard orchard? The revival of interest in orchards, noted in the last chapter, has led to the planting and restoration of many orchards. Many people or groups undertaking this work are new to the world of orchards. My involvement with the North Devon Orchards Campaign and later Orchards Live meant that I was approached for advice, and a course resulted.

People attending were surprised by the content which challenged some of their assumptions, and the feedback was positive. There is room here for only the briefest notes.

What is your orchard for? Fruit production was always listed, but other things were important. These days those aiming for large-scale fruit production quickly are unlikely to be planting standard orchards, and these notes are not for them. Just a few trees produce large amounts and so consider what the outlet will be – cider, juice, fruit, or a combination of these. For many people the question of 'traditional' varieties was a big issue.

Reasons other than fruit production were: historical, 'aesthetic', wildlife, cultural or 'recreational', and these had implications choice of rootstock (for size of tree) as much as varieties.

In planning there were a number of overlooked issues:

Management of the Sward: Essential after planting and subsequently, and for cider harvesting; stock or machine?

Boundary Fencing v Tree Guards: Guards will be essential if the sward under the trees is to be managed by stock.

Use of Fruit: Unless all for domestic use consider other users and their uses.

Resources: Most people had a monetary budget; time-planning is probably more important.

If these issues have been addressed those planting and restoring orchards should be better able to take advantage of the excellent advisory material that is available.

Appendix 2
Devon's Apple Varieties

There are 2000 apples from all over the world in Joan Morgan's classic *The Book of Apples*. The National Fruit Collection at Brogdale, near Faversham, Kent, is one of the largest fruit collections in the world; over 3500 named apples, pears, plums and cherries with bush fruits, vines and nuts. Most books are selective; H. V. Taylor had different volumes for different fruits, while the beautiful *The Apple Book* by Rosie Sanders is limited to 144 varieties.

In the 1990s the North Devon Save Our Orchards Campaign set up a Devon Pomona project with a published list of 'Devon Apples'. Volunteers nobly photographed specimens around Apple Day each year which were placed in an expanding folder. But the ongoing nature of the project pointed away from a finite published volume to a capacious website capable of addition and amendment. And this is what now exists, so I make no claim to offer a definitive list here, and refer you to www.devon-apples.co.uk

The website grows and develops each year, and it welcomes new information, and certainly new varieties. By the way, Devon-apples is a misnomer for other fruits are covered. There is a quite separate site for Exeter apples.

SOME APPLE VARIETY DESCRIPTIONS

Don's Delight. This apple, discovered as a seedling in a Torquay garden in the 1980s, was bought to the attention of Don Cockman, a Radio Devon presenter of gardening programmes. He took grafts, and in 1996 Kevin Croucher of Thornhayes Nurseries introduced it. It has vigorous growth, it is resistant to scab and canker (ideal for Devon), is pest-free (ideal for organic orchards), greenish flecked with red, and long-lasting. Quite a find!

Tidicombe Seedling. Named after a farm near Arlington in North Devon where it was found by early Save Our Orchards supporters Cheryl and Ed Thornburgh, beneath a window presumably from which its parent was thrown. Another Kevin Croucher introduction, and another apple ideal for Devon being resistant to scab and canker. The flesh is rich and the fruit lasts well past Wassails!

Brown's Apple. This was produced by Mr Hill, cider maker and nurserymen at Barkington, Staverton, probably around 1895 according to Liz Copas, and popularised in 1930s. Who were the Browns? An early high quality sharp apple, popular for planting in modern contract bush orchards; heavy cropper once established, but can be prone to biennialism.

Cockagee. This is the Irish name for 'goose terd'. The fruit is small and yellowish or olive green in colour. It has a Golden Pippin flavour and can make a single varietal cider. The story retold by James Crowden is that Sir William Courtenay of Powderham acquired an estate at Newcastle West in County Limerick following the defeat of the Desmonds in the reign of Elizabeth I. He (or his colonists) introduced this apple. It was brought back to Devon and Somerset two hundred years later as an Irish variety with an Irish name. Was common on Exmoor. (Cornwall and South West Fruit Focus, 2/1/2016.)

Devonshire Quarrenden (alternative spellings). This is one of Devon's oldest varieties, (mentioned in 1685 by John Ray, the naturalist), and was a highly praised and sought-after dessert apple, ready from late August. An attractive purply-red appearance, it is said to taste of strawberries but has a distinct flavour. But does it really crop as well as past descriptions?

Lucombe's Pine Raised in Lucombe & Pince's Nursery, Exeter, c1800. (Nursery also produced Lucombe's Seedling). It is aromatic and its strong acidity suggests pineapple. A good Christmas apple – golden, with the slightly freckled russeting like you see on Victorian Christmas table apples.

Steven's Woolbrook Pippin. Raised by Mr Stevens in his nursery in Sidmouth in 1903. According to the local paper he wanted to produce a Cox-like apple that did not suffer from canker. It is like a Cox with a coarser flesh.

Tom Putt. A conversation starter, or stopper, is to ask if Tom Putt is really a Devon apple? Nobody knows because Tom Putt lived near Honiton, and his nephew, the Reverend Tom Putt was rector of Trent (Dorset) having lived in Somerset! It can be used as a dessert, cooking or cider apple, so it is found in a lot of gardens where it has remarkable powers of rejuvenation accodrding to Liz Copas, and so the two things together explain why it is a variety that is so well known.

Tremlett's Bitter. Originating in the Exe Valley in the late nineteenth century this apple is probably the most significant in giving west country cider its reputation for astringency. It has a very red fruit that brightens the October orchard. It produces a full bittersweet cider – sweet juice but bitterly tannic.

Don's Delight. (Jane Pay)    *Lucombe's Pine.* (Jane Pay)    *Tom Putt.* (Jane Pay)    *Tremlett's Bitter.* (Jane Pay)

References

ALCOCK, N W: *An East Devon Manor*, TDA 102
ASTON, N and GERRARD, C: *Interpreting the English Village, Landscape and Community at Shapwick*, Windgather Press, 2013
BEECHAM, P: *Devon Buildings, An Introduction*, Devon Books, 2001
BENNETT, L S: *Life in the English Manor 1150-1400*, Cambridge UP, 1969
BRADBEER, J: *Early Victorian Farming on the Culm*, The Devon Historian, Vols 82, 84
BLAKE, W J: See Hooker's Synopsis Chorographical
BARRY, J: *Population Distribution and Growth* (in *Historical Atlas of SW England*, Exeter UP, 1999)
BRASSLEY, P et al: *English Countryside between the Wars*
CALDWELL, J: *A Provincial Horticultural Society*; TDA 92
CARUS-WILSON, E M: *The Expansion of Exeter at the Close of the Middle Ages*
CASELDENE, C J: *Environmental Setting* (in *Historical Atlas of SW England*, Exeter UP, 1999)
COLEPRESSE, S: *Georgicall Account of Devonshire and Cornwall*, 1667
COPAS, L: *Cider Apples, The New Pomona*, 2013
CURTLER, W H R: *A Short History of English Agriculture*, Oxford, 1909
DYER, C: *Making a Living in the Middle Ages*, Yale, 2002
EVANS, R: *Home Scenes*, Tavistock 1846
FINBERG, H P R: *Tavistock Abbey*, Cambridge UP, 1951
FOX, H S A: *Devon and Cornwall* (in *Agrarian History of E&W*, Cambridge UP, 1991)
FRASER, R: *General View of the County of Devon*, London, 1794
FREEMAN, R: *Dartmouth and Its Neighbours*, Phillimore, 1990
FRIEND, P: *Southern England*, Collins (New Naturalist), 2008
FUSSELL, G E: *Four Centuries of Farming Systems in Devon* 1500-1900, TDA 83
GRAY, T: *Devon Household Accounts, 1627-59, Part II*, DCRS 1996
HAGEN A: *Anglo-Saxon Food & Drink, Production & Distribution*, Anglo-Saxon Books, 1999
HAGGARD, H R: *Rural England*, Longman, 1902
HARDY, M: *Cider*, Devon Hist Soc Newsletter, 14, August 2014
HARVEY, D: *Fruit Growing in Kent in the Nineteenth Century*, Archaeologia Cantiana, vol 79
HERRING, P: *Fruit Growing and Market Gardening in the Tamar Valley* (for Tamar V AONB), 2003
HIGHAM, R: *Making Anglo-Saxon Devon*, Mint Press, 2008
HOOKER, J: *Synopsis Chorographical of Devonshire*
HOSKINS, W G: *Ownership and Occupation of Land in Devonshire*, 1650-1800, PhD thesis
JUNIPER, B E (and MABBERLEY, D J): *The Story of the Apple*, Timber Press, 2006
KEW, J in HAVINDEN, M: *The South West and the Land*, Exeter 1969
KOWALESKI, M: *Local Markets and Regional Trade in Medieval Exeter*, Cambridge, 1995

LANGLEY, B: *Pomona, A Curious Account of the Most Valuable Cider Fruit in Devonshire*
LAYCOCK, C H: *The Old Devon Farmhouse*, TDA 52, 54, 55,
LETHBRIDGE, R: *Apple Culture and Cider-Making in Devonshire*, TDA 1900
LYSONS, D & A: *Magna Britannia, Vol 6 Devon*, London, 1822
MacCAFFREY, W T: *Exeter 1540-1640, Growth of an English Country Town*, Harvard UP, 1975
MARSDEN, J: *Apples don't have Maggots*, Common Ground/English Nature, 1999
MARSHALL, W: *The Rural Economy of the West of England*, London
MAXTED, I: *Etched on Devon's Memory, Cider and 18th Cent Healthcare*, Exeter 1996
MINCHINTON, W: *Cider and Folklore*, Folk Life, Vol 13, 1975
NATURAL ENGLAND: *Research Report NERR025, Biodiversity Studies of Six Traditional Orchards*
OPPENHEIM, M M: *The Maritime History of Devon*, Exeter UP, 1968
PLANEL, P: *DHS Historical Orchards Project*, DHS Newsletter, February 2014
POLEWHELE, R: *The History of Devonshire*, London, 1806
POLLARD, E et al: *Hedges*, Collins New Naturalist, 1974
RHODES, M: *Devon's Torre Abbey*, The History Press, 2015
RISDON, T: *Choreographical Description*, London, 1811
ROACH, F A: *Cultivated Fruits of Britain*, Oxford, 1985
ROSEFF, R: *The Beginnings of Orchards*, www.archiveofciderpomology
SARSBY, J: *Sweetstone, Life on a Devon Farm*, Green Books, 2004
SIDMOUTH MUSEUM: Collected Papers (R & C Barnard)
STAFFORD, H: *Treatises on Cider*, 1755
STANES, R et al: *The Husbandry of Devon and Cornwall*, Stanes 2008
STANES, R: *Landlord and Tenant Husbandry in 18th Cent Devon*, Exeter Papers No 14
STOATE, T L (ed): *Survey of Country Manors 1525*, 1979
TANNER, H: *Farming of Devonshire*, 1848
TAYLOR, H V: *Plums of England*
THIRSK, J: *Alternative Agriculture, a History*, Oxford, 1997
TORR, C: *Small Talk at Wreyland*
TURNER, K C: *The Lost Orchards of Alfington*, Ottery St M Heritage Soc Journal, 2000,
TURNER S C: *Devon Historic Landscape Character*, Devon CC, 2005
UGAWA, K: *Economic Development of Devon Manors in 13th Cent*, TDA 44
UFFCULME LOCAL HISTORY GROUP: *A Culm Valley Parish*, Uffculme
VANCOUVER, C: *General View of the Agriculture of Devon*, 1808
WATKIN, H R: *Dartmouth*, Parochial Histories of Devonshire No 5, DA, 1935
WESTCOTE, T: *A View of Devonshire*, 1630
WILSON-NORTH, R (ed): *The Lie of the Land*, Mint Press 2003
WYATT, B: *Dartmouth Community Orchard Management Plan*, 2015
WYATT, P and STANES, R: *Uffculme: A Peculiar Parish*, Uffculme Archive Group ,1997
YOUINGS, J: *Devon Monastic Lands*, Devon and Cornwall Record Soc, New Series, Vol 1, 1955